Hope Restored

*The American Revolution and
the Founding of New Brunswick*

THE NEW BRUNSWICK MILITARY HERITAGE SERIES

Hope Restored

The AMERICAN REVOLUTION
and the Founding of
NEW BRUNSWICK

ROBERT L. DALLISON

The New Brunswick Military Heritage Series
Volume 2

GOOSE LANE EDITIONS
and
THE NEW BRUNSWICK MILITARY HERITAGE PROJECT

Edited by Lisa Alward.
Cover and interior design by Paul Vienneau and Julie Scriver.
NBMHP cartographer: Mike Bechthold.
Printed in Canada by Transcontinental.
10 9 8 7 6 5 4 3 2 1

Photos and other illustrative material on page 14 appear courtesy of the National Archives of Canada (NAC); on pages 18, 24, 36, 42, 52, 60, 66, 78, and 88, courtesy of the New Brunswick Museum (NBM); on pages 32, 40, 64, 80, 86, and 96, courtesy of Kings Landing Historical Settlement (KLHS); on page 84, courtesy of Heritage Resources, Saint John (HRSJ); on page 76, courtesy of the Provincial Archives of New Brunswick (PANB). Cover illustrations: Detail from *Illustrations of Uniforms of Loyalist Regiments of the American War of Independence*, NBM; detail from *A New and accurate map of the Islands of Newfoundland, Cape Briton, St. John and Anticosta . . . ,* 1747, by Emanuel Bowen, courtesy of the Bibliothèque nationale du Québec; detail from *Loyalists Landing at Saint John* by Adam Sheriff Scott, courtesy of the Cultural Affairs Office, City of Saint John.

NATIONAL LIBRARY OF CANADA CATALOGUING IN PUBLICATION

Dallison, Robert L., 1935-
    Hope restored: the American Revolution and the founding of New Brunswick /
    Robert L. Dallison.

(New Brunswick military heritage series; 2)
    Co-published by the New Brunswick Military Heritage Project.
Includes bibliographical references and index.
    ISBN 0-86492-371-6

    1. New Brunswick — History, Military. 2. Nova Scotia — History — 1775-1783.
    3. British — New Brunswick — History — 18th century. I. New Brunswick Military
    Heritage Project II. Title. III. Series.

FC2471.S34 2003   971.5'101   C2003-904747-4

Published with the financial support of the Canada Council for the Arts, the Government of Canada through the Book Publishing Industry Development Program, the New Brunswick Culture and Sports Secretariat, the Canadian War Museum, and the Military and Strategic Studies Program at the University of New Brunswick.

GOOSE LANE EDITIONS
469 King Street
Fredericton, New Brunswick
CANADA E3B 1E5
www.gooselane.com

NEW BRUNSWICK MILITARY HERITAGE PROJECT
Military and Strategic Studies Program
Department of History, University of New Brunswick
PO Box 4400
Fredericton NB E3C 1M4
www.unb.ca/nbmhp

*To the late Dr. George F.G. Stanley, historian and teacher,
who instilled in me a great love of Canadian history.*

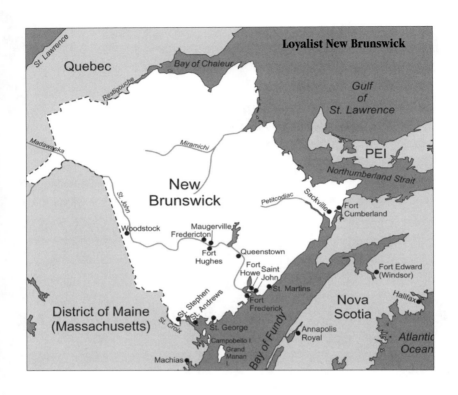

Loyalist New Brunswick

Quebec

Bay of Chaleur

St. Lawrence

Restigouche

Madawaska

Miramichi

New
Brunswick

St. John

Woodstock

Maugerville
Fredericton

Fort
Hughes

Queenstown

Fort
Howe
Saint
John

St. Martins

St. Stephen
St. Andrews

Fort
Frederick

St. Croix

St. George

Campobello I.

Grand
Manan
I.

Machias

District of Maine
(Massachusetts)

Gulf
of
St. Lawrence

PEI

Northumberland Strait

Petitcodiac

Sackville

Fort
Cumberland

Fort Edward
(Windsor)

Halifax

Nova
Scotia

Annapolis
Royal

Bay of Fundy

Atlantic
Ocean

TABLE OF CONTENTS

CHAPTER ONE

The Turmoil Spreads North

The American Revolutionary War Along the Bay of Fundy

The celebrated first shot of the American Revolutionary War was fired at Lexington, Massachusetts, on April 19, 1775. Almost immediately, reverberations were felt in what is now the Province of New Brunswick. The British garrisons at Fort Frederick, protecting the St. John River, and at Fort Cumberland, at the head of the Bay of Fundy, had been sent as reinforcements to Boston, to counter the growing unrest in British North America. When Captain Stephen Smith, a privateer from Machias in Massachusetts (now Maine), arrived at the mouth of the St. John River, he seized Fort Frederick without opposition, burned it to the ground, made prisoners of the four unfortunate remaining British soldiers, and captured the brig *Loyal Briton*. This vessel was loaded with provisions from the St. John River Valley. The poultry, cattle, and other much needed sup-

North view of Fort Frederick, built by Colonel Robert Monckton in 1758. Sketch by Captain Lieutenant Thomas Davies (detail). NATIONAL GALLERY OF CANADA

plies had been destined for the besieged British Army in Boston. Although the Bay of Fundy was on the periphery of British North America, the momentous events occurring in the Thirteen Colonies dragged the region into the American Revolutionary War; with the aftermath of the conflict defining New Brunswick and its future.

Following the Seven Years War, settlement along the Bay of Fundy was characterized by slow growth and a lagging economy. The region was very much a frontier; the settlers were still struggling to establish themselves, when this new war loomed on the horizon. With their exposed location and a population largely from New England, the Bay of Fundy settlements quickly attracted rebellious New Englanders endeavouring to enlist both the Native and non-Native populations in the rebel cause. The area suffered two invasions and num-erous raids during the war, with the outcome uncertain.

At the outbreak of the American Revolutionary War, the bound-aries of the British colony called Nova Scotia were ill defined. Nova Scotia certainly consisted of what are now the provinces of Nova Scotia, Prince Edward Island, and New Brunswick, but its northern border with Quebec and its western border with Massachusetts (now Eastern Maine), were subject to considerable debate. The defence of this extensive area fell to the British Royal Navy, but in 1775 the navy had a mere thirty ships in all the waters of North America. Only a few lightly armed sloops were available to protect Nova Scotia. How-ever, the uncontested raid on Fort Frederick had made it painfully obvious that the colony's shipping and its coast were easy prey for rebel raiders.

The British Army, besieged in Boston, was secure from direct as-sault, but it was effectively cut off from the surrounding countryside by George Washington's army. Soon it was in desperate need of all manner of supplies. Transporting goods from Britain was expensive and slow, but Nova Scotia offered an attractive alternative. Enterprising Nova Scotians quickly discerned that they could make handsome profits supplying the besieged British Army. Within two weeks, to the chagrin of the rebels sitting impatiently in their siege lines, over twenty vessels were bound for Boston, loaded with provisions. Rebel privateers reacted quickly, capturing a transport outside Boston Harbour fully laden with livestock from the Bay of Fundy. The Royal Navy responded by introducing a convoy system. Once ships were found for escort duty, the traffic from Nova Scotia continued unabated until Boston was evacuated.

Both the British and the rebels grasped Nova Scotia's strategic importance. In the summer of 1775 the colony was defended by only thirty-six regular soldiers who were fit for duty, and no British warships were permanently stationed in its waters. The fact that the vast majority of the inhabitants of Nova Scotia had come from the rebellious regions of New England within the last fifteen years heightened anxiety. In the autumn of 1775, the report of a force gathering on the Kennebec River under the command of Colonel Benedict Arnold intensified the fear of a rebel invasion. Massachusetts had advocated an attack on Nova Scotia, but the Continental Congress and General Washington opted for an invasion of Quebec, and that had become Arnold's objective. With this critical decision, the rebels lost the opportunity for an easy conquest of Nova Scotia.

The recognition of the defenceless state of Nova Scotia by King George III led to prompt corrective action. In October, 1775, two recently raised provincial corps, the Royal Fencible Americans and the 2nd Battalion of the Royal Highland Emigrants, arrived in Halifax from Boston. Reinforcements followed from Ireland under the command of General Eyre Massey, an experienced and respected army officer. Soon afterwards, a veteran naval officer, Commodore Marriot Arbuthnot, arrived from England to assume control of the Royal Dockyard in Halifax, and finally General Sir William Howe, the new commander-in-chief of the British Forces in North America, took a direct interest in the colony's defences.

As the unrest in British North America turned to rebellion, the sympathy of Nova Scotians became both mixed and volatile. There were staunch friends of the King, others who saw an advantage in supporting the royalist cause, dedicated rebels, others who advanced the need for political change but not rebellion, and those who only wished to be left alone. As Nova Scotia became embroiled in the conflict, settlers had to make very difficult choices, frequently with drastic results for themselves and their families. This bitter dilemma came to a head when rebels invaded the Bay of Fundy, aspiring to seize the British stronghold of Fort Cumberland.

Nova Scotians who espoused the rebel cause found haven in eastern Massachusetts in the District of Maine, particularly in the Port of Machias. From this sanctuary they plotted to free Nova Scotia from what they saw as British tyranny. Two prime instigators were Jonathan Eddy and John Allan, both prominent landowners on the Isthmus of Chignecto, in Cumberland County, and both former representatives in Nova Scotia's House of Assembly. When they failed to stir up a rebellion from within, they sought external support. Eddy appealed directly to Washington and to the Continental Congress; however, discouraged by their disastrous invasion of Quebec, they turned him down. The Colony of Massachusetts approved an assault on Fort Cumberland but committed only to a promise of some supplies. With this meagre blessing, Eddy set about raising an army.

In May, 1776, New England privateers reappeared on the St. John River, penetrating eighty-five kilometres up the river to Maugerville, an agricultural community established twelve years earlier by settlers from Essex County, Massachusetts. The privateers warned of an impending invasion and predicted a rebel victory, when all those who did not actively support the rebel cause would lose their land. Ten-

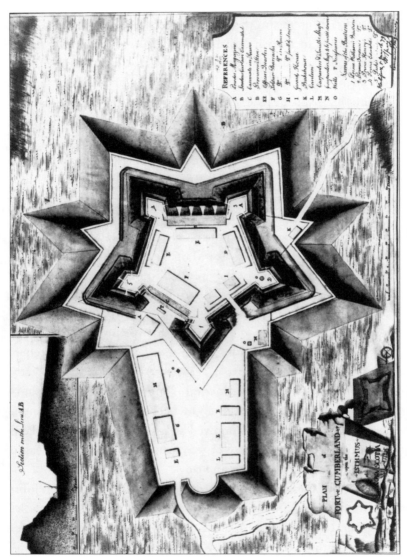

Plan of Fort Cumberland, *by William Spry (1778)*. NAC, C-34708

sion grew when the local natives, the Maliseet, threatened suspected "Tories." This tipped the balance in favour of the rebels, and the citizens of Maugerville signed a formal declaration of allegiance to the Continental Congress and proclaimed their community a part of Massachusetts. The more circumspect inhabitants at the mouth of the St. John River, on the other hand, avoided making any public declaration. This set the stage for the arrival in Saint John Harbour of Colonel Eddy's invasion force, which consisted of twenty-eight men from Machias and another seven from Campobello Island in Passamaquoddy Bay. The rebels failed to attract recruits from the community at Portland Point in the Saint John Harbour, but they did obtain twenty-seven recruits from Maugerville, as well as sixteen Maliseet under Chief Ambroise St. Aubin. Eddy was disappointed, as he had expected a better response from the Maliseet and support from the Acadian communities along the St. John River Valley. Nevertheless, buoyed by republican zeal and determination, the invasion force, now seventy-two men strong, set off up the Bay of Fundy in late October, 1776, in open whaleboats and canoes.

After months of unsettling rumours, the British had assumed that by October the invasion season was over. They relaxed their guard, permitting Eddy and his men to capture a small outpost on Shepody Bay and to seize the British sloop *Polly*, loaded to the delight of Eddy and his men, with winter clothes and provisions. These initial successes helped to attract twenty-two Acadians from the area and enough recruits from the settlers of Cumberland County to bring the rebel force to approximately 200 men. Eddy was now poised to attack Fort Cumberland, the star-shaped fortification overlooking the Tantramar Marsh.

Unfortunately for the rebels, the opportunity for an easy victory had passed. When General Howe and the British Army evacuated

Boston on St. Patrick's Day, 1776, they sailed to Halifax. Although they remained only until June, Howe was able to obtain first-hand knowledge and an appreciation of the situation in Nova Scotia. He directed that control of the St. John River be retained, that a detachment of 100 soldiers from the Royal Highland Emigrants be stationed at Fort Edward, in Windsor, and that Fort Cumberland become the British stronghold in the Bay of Fundy area. He appointed Lieutenant-Colonel Joseph Goreham of the Royal Fencible Americans as commander of Fort Cumberland, with a garrison of 200 men from his regiment.

Goreham and his men arrived on June 4 and immediately set to work repairing Fort Cumberland's fortifications, restoring the barracks, and arming it with three 9-pounder and three 6-pounder cannons. When the rebels appeared, the repairs were still incomplete, the water source was not secure, supplies and fuel were limited, and the garrison, having lost sixty-three men in the initial encounters with Eddy's rebels, was reduced to 172 Fencibles and four gunners from the Royal Artillery. The recently recruited Fencibles were untrained and lacked proper clothing. In these circumstances, Goreham concluded that it would be unwise to be adventuresome and opted to remain on the defence, safe behind the fort's walls.

The rebel force set up camp on Mount Whatley, behind Fort Cumberland. Then, in accordance with custom, Eddy formally demanded the surrender of the fort. Goreham, assessing his opponent's strength, boldly responded by suggesting Eddy surrender to him. On November 12, the rebels attempted a night assault using scaling ladders, but the garrison beat them back with artillery and musket fire. A week later, the rebels attacked again, with the aim of setting fire to the exposed powder magazine. They successfully set the barracks alight, but the fire did not spread to the magazine, and the garrison once again repelled the attackers. Reluctantly, Eddy concluded that he could not take the fort by assault and settled down for a siege.

Once news of Eddy's invasion reached Halifax, the British reacted swiftly. They sent reinforcements overland to Windsor and arranged transport to move them from there by sea to Fort Cumberland. To Goreham's great relief, on November 26, ships carrying companies of the British Marines and the Royal Highland Emigrants appeared off Fort Cumberland. A surprise night attack on the rebel camp dispersed the invaders. Fort Cumberland and Nova Scotia were to remain British strongholds for the remainder of the war.

With some exceptions, Goreham offered a general amnesty to all local rebels, and he put an end to acts of vengeance by loyal settlers, who had taken to looting and burning rebel farms. It was time for healing, but the hurt was deep, and the community remained bitterly divided for years to come. Meanwhile, Eddy's defeated force fled overland to the St. John River in bitter winter weather, without food or warm clothing. In their desperation, they took merciless revenge on anyone they encountered along the way. After seizing supplies at Portland Point, the rebels spent a miserable winter in Maugerville before returning to Machias.

In early January, 1777, John Allan received a positive response to a more ambitious proposal for an invasion of Nova Scotia. Thanks to Allan's oratorical skills and the fading memories of the unsuccessful Quebec campaign, the Continental Congress directed Massachusetts to raise 3,000 men at Continental expense to seize Fort Cumberland and destroy the dockyard at Halifax. This time it was Massachusetts that lacked enthusiasm. After appointing Allan to the rank of colonel, the colony approved the raising of only a single regiment in eastern Maine, with the limited task of occupying the St. John River Valley. Allan was also appointed the Superintendent of Eastern Indians,

Fort Howe /78/

Sketch of Fort Howe, by Benjamin Marston (1781). This is a photograph taken around 1910 of the Marston sketch. NBM

with the task of bringing the Passamaquoddy and Maliseet peoples into the rebel fold. Recruiting proved slow and difficult. Before he was ready, Allan learned that a British force had once again reappeared in the St. John River Valley.

After Fort Cumberland was relieved, the Nova Scotia Government sent Colonel Arthur Goold on HMS *Vulture* to the St. John River and Maugerville to re-establish British control. By mid-May, with the support of a military detachment under the command of Brigade Major Gilfred Studholme, Goold had induced the majority of the inhabitants to swear an oath of allegiance to the Crown. Upon hearing that Goold and HMS *Vulture* had left, Colonel Allan immediately sailed from Machias to Saint John Harbour with a force of forty-three men. On June 1, 1777, he landed at Manawagonish Cove and attacked Portland Point from the rear. The rebels took the leading citizens prisoner and seized their goods. Following the arrival of another forty men, Colonel Allan left half his force to secure the harbour and took the other half and his prisoners up river to hold talks with the Maliseet.

British authorities in Halifax reacted promptly to the news of Allan's activities by dispatching another force to the St. John River in late June, 1777. This force consisted of the warships *Mermaid*, *Vulture*, and *Hope* and a detachment of soldiers under the command of Brigade Major Studholme. HMS *Vulture*, the first to arrive, attempted unsuccessfully to land at Portland Point. Then Studholme and 120 Provincials landed at Manawagonish Cove, skirmished with the rebels and put them to flight. The British hotly pursued the rebels up the river, but they fled, along with Allan and his group, back to Machias by way of Eel River and the St. Croix Lakes. Those Maliseet who had supported the rebel cause decamped for Maine as well, while the remainder under Chief Pierre Tomah reaffirmed their allegiance. The British then withdrew to Halifax, leaving the St. John River Valley defenceless yet again. A ruthless rebel privateer with the colourful name of Captain Agreen Crabtree quickly took advantage of the situation. With his eight-gun sloop, the *Molly and Hannah*, Crabtree attacked Portland Point, carrying off twenty-one boatloads of loot and molesting the inhabitants to such an extent that many abandoned their homes. A desperate appeal was made to the authorities in Halifax for long-term protection.

The British authorities finally recognized the need for a more permanent solution and ordered Brigade Major Studholme to secure the mouth of the St. John River. He arrived back in Saint John Harbour in November, 1777, with fifty hand-picked men, a pre-fabricated blockhouse, and four 6-pounder cannons. The armed sloop that transported them remained all winter as added protection. Studholme opted not to rebuild Fort Frederick on the west side of the harbour, but to erect a new fort on a strategically located hill on the

Painting of the Loyalists landing at Saint John, by Adam Sheriff Scott.
CULTURAL AFFAIRS OFFICE, CITY OF SAINT JOHN

east side. Located above the site of the old Fort La Tour, Fort Howe commanded a splendid view of the whole harbour. With the help of local citizens, the garrison set to work immediately, and by mid-winter of 1777-1778 they had reassembled the blockhouse, constructed defensive works, and built snug winter quarters. When the notorious privateer Captain Crabtree returned later that winter, he was astonished to find the harbour defended. To the relief of the local inhabitants, he quietly sailed away.

Fort Howe consolidated British control over the St. John River for the remainder of the war, just as Fort Cumberland secured the fertile agricultural area at the head of the Bay of Fundy. However, rebel privateering continued to pose a serious threat to coastal communities. The informal type of warfare known as privateering appealed to New Englanders. A privateer was a privately owned armed vessel licensed by a letter of marque to prey on the commerce of a country's enemies. All captured vessels and their cargo could be sold for the benefit of the owners and crew. With this promise of easy wealth, rebel privateers of all shapes and sizes flooded into Nova Scotian waters and the Gulf of St. Lawrence. By the end of 1776, privateers had captured nearly 350 British vessels. They had sacked most of the settlements along the Nova Scotian coast and devastated the north shore fishery. It was not all one-sided, however, as HMS *Wolf* and HMS *Diligence* intercepted rebel privateers raiding the Bay of Chaleur and sunk two off Percé Rock. Captain Harvey, commander of HMS *Viper*, captured three privateers in the Bay of Fundy, as well as the privateer *Lafayette* on the way to the Miramichi. Captain James Dawson in the speedy, black-hulled sloop HMS *Hope* earned a reputation as a particularly effective privateer hunter. Consequently, by the end of 1776, the Royal Navy had gained some control over the rebel privateers and with this added sense of security came a swing in Nova Scotian sympathy to the Loyalist cause. Not surprisingly, the British authorities also issued letters of marque, and Nova Scotians were soon excelling in the art of privateering. Although uncertainty and alarms continued, the colony was able to take full advantage of the many commercial opportunities offered by a war economy. Nova Scotians would remember the war as a period of prosperity.

Although a frontier society, Nova Scotia was part of British North America and could not avoid participation in the American Revolutionary War. Its strategic position ensured that it was actively involved from the very beginning of the conflict, and Nova Scotians were compelled to choose sides. Had the rebels assigned its conquest a higher priority, Nova Scotia could have easily become the fourteenth rebel colony. As the war unfolded, it became clear that the colony would be part of a new British Empire in North America. At war's end, a new international boundary had to be defined and secured, and the plight of thousands of refugees who had supported the British King had to be resolved.

CHAPTER TWO

In the Service of King George III

The British Provincial Corps and Their Arrival in New Brunswick

Despite the chaos caused by rebel invasions and incursions, Nova Scotia remained under British control at the conclusion of the American Revolutionary War. Although the western frontier remained ill defined, it had been protected in the final phase of the conflict by the British occupation of Castine and the Penobscot Valley. A sizable Loyalist community had settled around Castine in the expectation that a new British colony would be established along the Penobscot River to the west of Nova Scotia. These aspirations were dashed when the eastern border of the United States was set along the St. Croix River. The desire to firmly fix and secure the new boundary prompted Sir Guy Carleton, the British commander-in-chief, to settle the bulk of the British provincial corps in the St. John River Valley. The men of these regiments, having openly demonstrated their allegiance by

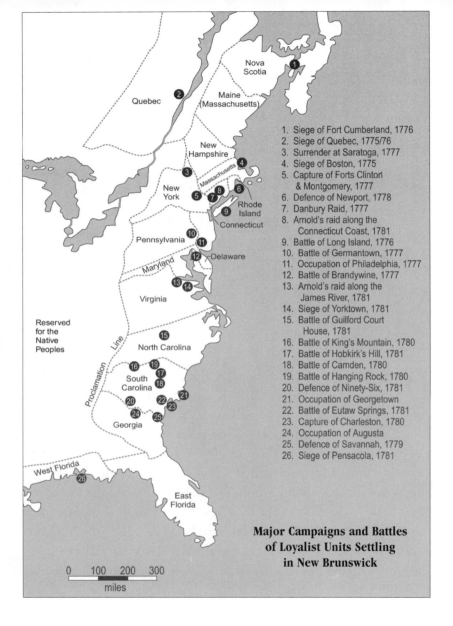

1. Siege of Fort Cumberland, 1776
2. Siege of Quebec, 1775/76
3. Surrender at Saratoga, 1777
4. Siege of Boston, 1775
5. Capture of Forts Clinton & Montgomery, 1777
6. Defence of Newport, 1778
7. Danbury Raid, 1777
8. Arnold's raid along the Connecticut Coast, 1781
9. Battle of Long Island, 1776
10. Battle of Germantown, 1777
11. Occupation of Philadelphia, 1777
12. Battle of Brandywine, 1777
13. Arnold's raid along the James River, 1781
14. Siege of Yorktown, 1781
15. Battle of Guilford Court House, 1781
16. Battle of King's Mountain, 1780
17. Battle of Hobkirk's Hill, 1781
18. Battle of Camden, 1780
19. Battle of Hanging Rock, 1780
20. Defence of Ninety-Six, 1781
21. Occupation of Georgetown
22. Battle of Eutaw Springs, 1781
23. Capture of Charleston, 1780
24. Occupation of Augusta
25. Defence of Savannah, 1779
26. Siege of Pensacola, 1781

Major Campaigns and Battles of Loyalist Units Settling in New Brunswick

bearing arms for the King, ensured a staunchly loyal population on the frontier. This unique settlement pattern was a key factor in the formation of the Province of New Brunswick.

The signing of the Treaty of Paris on September 3, 1783, ended the American Revolutionary War, and launched Nova Scotia into its historic role of providing sanctuary for thousands of Loyalist refugees. While the colony was already an asylum for those fleeing rebel persecution, it was not until October, 1782, that large numbers of refugees began appearing, some 300 arriving in the Annapolis Valley and others filling Halifax to capacity. The real onslaught was still to come. Sir Guy Carleton was under immense pressure. He had to evacuate New York immediately, but he was also scrambling to evacuate Charleston, South Carolina, and the Penobscot River Valley. British regular troops and German mercenaries had to be returned to Europe, and military operations were continuing in the West Indies. There was simply insufficient transport to meet the demand, and it would take more than a year before the last refugee and British soldier left New York City on November 25, 1783.

Although the Treaty of Paris promised the Loyalists a safe return to their pre-war homes, persecution of "Tories" escalated with the rebel victory. The *New Hampshire Gazette* reported with delight that a Loyalist had been seized in his hometown of Boothbay. His unforgiving former neighbours placed a halter around his neck, hoisted him up a masthead with a crowbar under his crotch, and left him to dangle from 8 o'clock in the morning until noon the following day. After promising never to return, the unfortunate man was clamped in irons and shipped back to British territory. Such tales encouraged the Loyalists to seek refuge outside of the United States. The Loyalists who had served in the British Army had the most to fear from a vengeful America. During the war numerous provincial corps fought alongside British regulars. These Loyalist regiments had served in

Oil portrait of Colonel John Murray (detail), by John Singleton Copley. In 1776, the rebels damaged the portrait with a sabre slash to the head.
NBM

many capacities and in all theatres of war. As the conflict slowly drew to a close, with the capitulation at Yorktown and the evacuation of Charleston, the Provincials gathered around New York City and on Long Island. Half of the refugees who settled in New Brunswick were disbanded soldiers from these provincial corps and their families.

Fourteen blocks of land were laid out from Maugerville northward along the St. John River to what is now Woodstock for the provincial corps, with two additional blocks along the Fundy coast. Since the British military believed that the Treaty of Paris would prove to be only a temporary armistice and that hostilities could recommence at any time, each block was assigned to a specific regiment. The idea behind settling the provincial corps in regimental blocks along the frontier, with their officers and men intact, was to facilitate their quick assembly in time of war. A ribbon of habitation soon developed along the lower portion of the St. John River, with the Sussex Vale, the Kingston Peninsula, Gagetown, and Fredericton forming population centres. Fifteen of the provincial corps were settled along the St. John River Valley, while other Loyalist regiments received land grants elsewhere in the Maritime Provinces. For example, the British Legion, headquarters personnel, and others were allocated land in Port Mouton, Nova Scotia. Most soon left that desolate area to seek better opportunities elsewhere. Among them was Captain Nehemiah Marks of the Armed Boatmen, who sailed with 280 followers to Passamaquoddy Bay and the St. Croix River to found the town of St. Stephen.

Back on Long Island as the Loyalists waited impatiently for transportation, the idea took root of a separate and distinct province for those of proven loyalty. This would be a just reward for their suffering and loss on behalf of the Crown. Support for the concept grew once the Loyalists arrived in Nova Scotia. In their view, the men who governed Nova Scotia were of questionable loyalty and had unjustly prospered from the war. The "real" Loyalists on the other hand, had incurred only misfortune. Governor John Parr and his government seemed determined to frustrate Loyalist aspirations and assigned them the most isolated and barren parts of the province. When rumours abounded that Parr was planning to dissolve the House of Assembly and hold an election before the newly arrived Loyalists could qualify for the franchise, the demand for a separate Loyalist province gained momentum. With the support of Sir Guy Carleton, the proposal won approval in London. The first area considered was along the Penobscot River, around the British stronghold of Castine and its neighbouring Loyalist settlement, with New Ireland suggested as a name. This proposal was eliminated when the international border was located on St. Croix River. The final resolution saw the creation of New Brunswick on June 18, 1784. Since the majority of Loyalists had a military connection with strong, well-developed ties of comradeship and cooperation, they quickly took

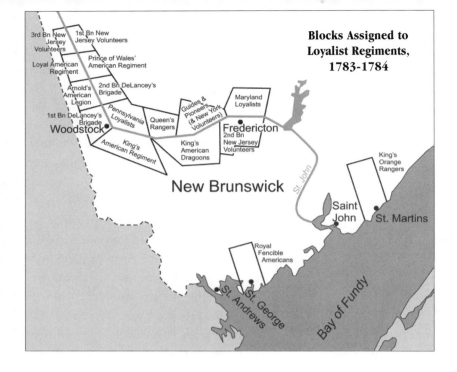

Blocks Assigned to Loyalist Regiments, 1783-1784

control of the shaping and development of the new province. It was these military Loyalists who gave New Brunswick the motto of *Spem Reduxit* — Latin for "Hope Restored."

The British Army consisted of three different types of military units: the British regulars, the militia, and the provincial corps. Representatives from all three settled in New Brunswick. The British regulars were professional soldiers who usually served for life. They were well trained, disciplined, experienced, and led by dedicated professional officers. Seldom equalled on the battlefield, the regulars were the offensive arm of the British Army. At the war's end, they were either reassigned elsewhere within the British Empire or disbanded. Some regulars took their release in North America. A de tailed return, dated September, 1783, shows that 1,144 soldiers from sixteen different regular regiments were disbanded in Nova Scotia, along with 429 women and children. Of this group 384 soldiers, with 146 women and children, came to the St. John River Valley. The largest group of regulars to settle in New Brunswick were Highlanders from the 42nd Regiment (the Black Watch), who took up land along the Nashwaak River.

Traditionally, in British North America, the colonial militia were responsible for local defence in times of emergency. The militiaman was a part-time soldier, who was usually expected to arm and equip himself. Generally poorly trained and badly led, he was not expected to serve outside his home territory. When the Revolution started, the rebels were quick to seize control of the militia and its resources. It was a rebel-controlled militia that fought the British regulars at Lexington, and the British objective at Concord was to secure contested militia stores. Once the British realized that the rebellion would not be quickly suppressed, they attempted to reform the militia in those areas under their control. With varying degrees of success, they re-established militia units in New York City, on Long Island, in Nova Scotia, in Georgia, and in the Carolinas. The militia routinely performed garrison duties. In May, 1780, for example, 100 militiamen worked on the Citadel Hill fortifications in Halifax. Some militia units achieved notable successes. In 1780, the Lunenburg Militia of Nova Scotia captured two rebel privateers; the Brig *Sally*, commanded by Master Moses Tinney, and the Brig *Kitty*, commanded by Master John Palmer. The Westchester Refugees, under the command of Colonel James Delancey, was extremely effective. This militia regiment controlled large portions of Westchester County, New York, and helped supply the British Army with fresh provisions. Militia service could be costly, as Nathan Davison

The coat of arms of New Brunswick. The galley represents the ships which brought the Loyalists to the province. The motto, translated, is "Hope Restored." COMMUNICATIONS NEW BRUNSWICK

discovered. Seriously wounded in the pursuit of a rebel privateer that had captured a schooner full of refugees in the Minas Basin, Davison returned home so crippled that he was unable to support his wife and six children. The militia also tasted bitter defeat at the battle of King's Mountain in South Carolina in October, 1780. Because they had fought for the King, many militiamen had no option at war's end but to flee.

The soldiers in the provincial corps differed from the British regulars and the militiamen. Provincials were recruited in North America for service anywhere within the region, and enlisted on a full-time basis for the duration of the conflict. They were organized, armed, and trained much like the British regulars. The British issued warrants to men of social stature (frequently veterans of the Seven Years War), authorizing them to raise regiments. Leading Loyalists like Oliver DeLancey, Sir Courtland Skinner, Edmund Fanning, and Sir William Johnston, were among those selected. They were responsible for nominating their officers and recruiting the men. Success depended on influential contacts, deep pockets to cover expenses, and substantial luck. Recruiting was especially challenging and dangerous, because the rebels did everything in their power to prevent their compatriots from joining the British Army. When Captain Moses Dunbar returned to his Connecticut hometown of Waterbury to enlist men for his company of the King's American Regiment, the rebels apprehended him. He escaped, only to be recaptured and publicly hanged on the grounds of Trinity College, Hartford, on March 9, 1777.

A provincial corps normally consisted of one battalion, though DeLancey's Brigade had three battalions, and at one point the New Jersey Volunteers had six. The authorized strength of a battalion was normally 500 men, divided into ten companies. (Major Timothy Hierlihy, however, received approval to raise only five companies for his corps). Initially, almost all provincial regiments wore green uniform coats with different coloured trim or facings, but starting in the 1778 campaign, they were granted the privilege of wearing the scarlet uniforms of the British regulars. While most Provincials proudly accepted the red uniforms, some, like the Queen's Rangers and Emmerick's Chasseurs, retained the green ones as a point of honour. Each provincial regiment was unique with its own record of achievements, experiences, and sense of pride. The brotherhood developed during the war, as with all veterans, produced very close relationships, which lasted long after the regiment was disbanded. These relationships played an important role in the development of New Brunswick.

The British commander-in-chief, Howe, selected a number of talented Loyalists to help administer the expanding provincial corps.

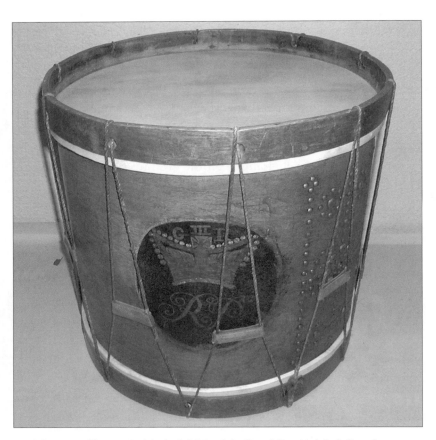

A drum, emblazoned with the initials of the Royal Provincials, believed to have been carried by the British Legion during the American Revolutionary War. KLHS

He made Alexander Innes Inspector General of Provincial Forces with the rank of lieutenant-colonel. To establish financial control, he appointed Colonel Edward Winslow Muster Master General of the Provincial Forces, with the task of mustering each regiment six times a year so that every soldier could be paraded, counted, and identified. (These muster lists are now invaluable aids to military and family historians.) Winslow was eventually assisted by deputy-muster masters, including his old friend Ward Chipman. Both Winslow and Chipman settled in Fredericton where they became actively involved in the affairs of the new colony.

The British military authorities were slow to accept the provin-cial corps as equals, causing dissatisfaction among the Loyalists and dampening their enthusiasm. Regular officers had precedence over Provincial officers regardless of seniority. When it came to issuing new equipment or clothing or assigning quarters, the British regulars always appeared to be favoured. The Provincials also believed they were given the more routine or mundane military tasks. The Royal Fencible Americans, for example, felt insulted when employed as fishermen to feed the Halifax Garrison, and the Royal Highland Emigrants resented being used on privateers and navy auxiliary vessels. Moreover, there were no provisions for medical services, pensions for widows, or support for Provincials wounded in action. It was not until 1779 that the British finally recognized the potential of the Provincials and improved their conditions of service. Provincial regiments that achieved a suitable standard of efficiency and a full complement of men could now be placed on the British regular establishment or on the newly instituted American regular establishment, guaranteeing their officers a pension, known as half pay, after the war. The Royal Highland Emigrants were placed on the British establishment as the 84th Regiment of Foot. Five other regiments were placed on the American regular establishment: the Queen's

Rangers, the Volunteers of Ireland, the New York Volunteers, the King's American Regiment, and the British Legion. Representatives from all these regiments settled in New Brunswick.

Provincial regiments were raised across British North America, from Canada to Nova Scotia to Florida. The largest number, however, was raised in New York, New Jersey, and Connecticut, following Howe's victory over Washington in the battle of White Plains on September 28, 1776. Success in raising regiments varied widely, with failure not unknown. George Wightman was authorized to raise a provincial regiment on Rhode Island. But the British withdrawal from Rhode Island cut Wightman off from his recruiting base and his unit peaked at eighty-two men. Major William Stark, the older brother of the successful and renowned rebel General John Stark, obtained a warrant to raise a unit to be called the New Hampshire Volunteers, but he failed completely. Despite the difficulties, recruiting continued throughout the war. A strength return for the provincial corps under the command of Howe, dated November, 1777, reported a force of 311 officers, 280 sergeants, ninety-four drummers, and 3,797 soldiers. In December, 1780, the provincial corps reached its maximum strength of 9,659 men. This figure, however, does not include two battalions of the Royal Highland Emigrants (with a strength of over 1,000), recently placed on the British establishment, two newly formed regiments, or several units outside the control of the Central Department in New York. In January, 1783, the British Army under the command of Sir Guy Carleton had a total strength of 33,479 men, of which 8,117 were Provincials. It has been estimated that approximately 21,000 men saw service in the provincial corps, a figure which compares favourably with the strength of Washington's Continental Army.

The provincial corps served with courage and distinction. They formed a major component of the New York garrison and provided regiments for the defence of Nova Scotia, Quebec, and the West Indies. They served in the Philadelphia Campaign of 1777, where during the battle of Brandywine the Queen's Rangers earned a reputation for discipline and daring. Provincial corps also participated in the successful defence of Rhode Island and Savannah, facing a combined French and rebel army. Under General Sir Henry Clinton, they captured the Hudson River strongholds of Forts Montgomery and Clinton. They destroyed a major rebel supply depot during the Danbury Raid, and participated in raids along the Connecticut coast, as well as in New Jersey and the Mohawk Valley of New York. The Provincials were prominent throughout the Southern Campaign, making up about a third of the British force. They played key roles in the capture of Savannah, Augusta, and Charleston; garrisoned numerous back-country posts; and fought in the battles of Camden, the Cowpens, Guilford Court House, Hobkirk's Hill, Ninety-Six, and Eutaw Springs. When France, Spain, and Holland entered the conflict, Provincials helped garrison the British West Indies; fought the Spanish at Pensacola, West Florida; attacked Fort San Juan in Nicaragua; and captured New Providence in the Bahamas.

The American Revolutionary War dragged on for eight weary years. While the surrender of the British under Cornwallis at Yorktown in October, 1781, did not stop the fighting, it gave a clear indication of the eventual outcome. To the very end, the Provincial Forces continued to support the Crown with courage, determination, and fortitude. A grateful King George III sought to acknowledge this impressive record of service won at great personal sacrifice. His fulfillment of this obligation would have a direct impact on New Brunswick.

*A private soldier of DeLancey's Brigade,
as depicted in* Illustration of Uniforms
of Loyalist Regiments of the American
War of Independence. NBM

CHAPTER THREE

The Loyalist Regiments

The Provincial Corps Disbanded in New Brunswick

Approval was given to raise up to seventy provincial corps within British North America during the course of the American Revolutionary War. Some of these regiments achieved considerable fame, while others failed to evolve. Members of the following regiments played a prominent role in the founding and settlement of New Brunswick.

American Legion

When the Continental General Benedict Arnold defected to the British, he received authority to raise a provincial corps called the American Legion, with a warrant to recruit from among the ranks of Continental Army deserters. The maximum strength Arnold was able to obtain was 212 men, which was far short of a full strength corps of 500. The officers came from New York City and from the Loyalist camps on Long Island, and included two young lieutenants of cavalry; twelve-year-old Richard Arnold and nine-year-old Henry Arnold. Always a devoted family man, Arnold ensured his sons' financial future by commissioning them into his regiment. After the war, as commissioned officers, Richard and Henry received half pay for the remainder of their lives. Arnold himself received the rank of brigadier-general in the British forces, one rank lower than the rank he had held in the Continental Army

Arnold was always a controversial and difficult man, but his first love was military service, and he proved to be as effective a commander for the British as he had been for the rebels. In December, 1780, he led an expeditionary force of 1,000 men, including the American Legion and the Queen's Rangers, to the James River in Virginia. The purpose was to rally Virginian Loyalists and to destroy rebel supplies being collected at Richmond and Petersburg. By June, 1781, after creating considerable havoc, Arnold and the American Legion were back in New York. In September, 1781, he commanded a 1,700-man raiding force that successfully attacked rebel privateering bases at New London and Groton in Connecticut. The American Legion captured Fort Trumbull and helped sack New London. Arnold's regiment ended the war as part of the New York garrison. A return dated September, 1783, shows that a total of 112 officers, men, women, children, and servants from the American

Legion had embarked for the St. John River Valley. They were allocated block number ten in the parish of Wakefield.

DeLancey's Brigade

A captain in the British regular army, Oliver DeLancey came from a prominent New York family. General Sir William Howe was directed by authorities in London to appoint DeLancey a brigadier-general empowered to raise a provincial corps consisting of a brigade of up to four battalions. His warrant specified that the corps be employed "for the defence of Long Island and other exigencies." At its peak, DeLancey's Brigade consisted of three battalions, recruited mainly from communities on Long Island, with the 3rd Battalion composed solely of men from Queens County. The brigade formed part of the New York garrison; the 3rd Battalion never served off Long Island. When General Parson, a notorious rebel whaleboat privateer, attacked Setauket on Long Island, Lieutenant-Colonel Richard Hewlett and the 3rd Battalion successfully defended their post in a fortified church. Hewlett and his men received commendation for their "spirited behaviour and good conduct."

In November, 1778, the 1st and 2nd Battalions sailed to East Florida to serve in the Southern Campaign. The 1st Battalion helped inflict severe casualties on the combined French and rebel force which attempted to storm Savannah in 1779. Both battalions participated in the capture of Charleston, and the 2nd Battalion was part of the garrison that withstood the siege of Fort Ninety-Six in South Carolina. They also both fought at the battle of Eutaw Springs. Due to heavy losses, the 1st and 2nd Battalions were combined in February, 1782.

*The drum carried by the Guides and Pioneers during the American
Revolutionary War.* KLHS

After the war, what remained of DeLancey's Brigade sailed for the St. John River. The 1st Battalion was allocated block number eight in the parish of Woodstock, and the renumbered 2nd Battalion received block number nine in the parish of Northampton. Colonel Hewlett petitioned the governor to exchange block nine (which he considered too difficult of access) for block seven where there were still vacant lots. While waiting impatiently for an official response, many soldiers and their families settled lower down the river in the counties of Queens and Sunbury.

Guides and Pioneers

The Guides and Pioneers were raised in New York City on the orders of Sir William Howe in the autumn of 1776. A combat unit with the specialized functions of guiding, building fortifications, and improving lines of communication, detachments of the Guides and Pioneers participated in all operations and theatres of war. The Philadelphia Campaign, the siege of Newport, Rhode Island, the Southern Campaign, and the assaults on Forts Montgomery and Clinton are just some of the operations supported by the Guides and Pioneers. The unit served as part of the New York garrison, on raids into New Jersey, and accompanied Arnold during his raid along the Connecticut coast. A return of troops on the eve of the battle of Camden reveals that Cornwallis's force included one lieutenant, three sergeants, and twenty-three Pioneers. Lieutenant Angus McDonald was wounded in this battle, and two Pioneers were killed. In September, 1783, fourteen officers, nine sergeants, two drummers, seventy-five soldiers, thirty-two women, fifty-six children, and fifteen servants — a total of 203 people — embarked for the St. John River

The guidon of the King's American Dragoons, presented to the regiment by William, Prince of Wales, in 1782. NBM

Valley. The Guides and Pioneers, along with the New York Volunteers, were allocated block number three in the parishes of Bright and Queensbury.

King's American Dragoons

In January, 1779, Lord George Germain, the British Secretary of State for the American Department, directed that his secretary, Major Benjamin Thompson, receive a lieutenant-colonel's commission in the British regular army and a warrant to raise a provincial corps in

America. Born in Woburn, Massachusetts, Thompson taught school in Rumford (now Concord, New Hampshire) and served as a major in the militia, before being forced to flee rebel persecution. When the British Army evacuated Boston, he sailed to London and joined Germain's staff. The newly promoted Thompson arrived first in Charleston, South Carolina, where General Alexander Leslie placed him in command of a detachment tasked to hunt Colonel Francis Marion, the famous rebel guerrilla leader, known as the "Swamp Fox." Thompson succeeded in driving Marion and his band into the wasteland along the Santee River and then sailed to New York to take command of the King's American Dragoons.

When a proposal was presented to form a mounted regiment, combining a number of small independent provincial corps in the New York area, Germain gave consent and appointed his protégé as commander. In February, 1781, the regiment was organized with six troops, each consisting of three officers, two sergeants, two corporals, one trumpeter, one farrier, and fifty-five troopers. The Volunteers of New England were incorporated into the Dragoons, and its commander Joshua Upham, a friend of Thompson's, was appointed major. Captain Daniel Murray of the Wentworth Volunteers was appointed second major. By January, 1782, Leslie reported that several detached corps of cavalry had been incorporated into the Dragoons under Lieutenant-Colonel Thompson, whose guidance had produced a "respectable" unit. Thompson proudly wrote that the regiment had 388 effectives on strength, surpassing the authorized establishment of 366 men. Later, the regiment included four field cannons for a troop of "flying artillery." On August 1, 1782, William, Prince of Wales, who was a midshipman on a visiting warship, presented the King's American Dragoons with its regimental flag in a formal ceremony near Flushing on Long Island. This flag, called a guidon, survives in the collection of the New Brunswick Museum.

The Dragoons operated as part of the New York garrison, working in conjunction with other mounted units. A return shows that 267 men, forty-five women, fifty-two children, and forty servants embarked for the St. John River Valley. The Dragoons arrived with the spring fleet and were allocated block number four, in the parish of Prince William, named for the regiment's patron. The last formal review of the King's American Dragoons was held in Prince William on October 10, 1783.

King's American Regiment (4th American Regiment)

On December 11, 1776, Sir William Howe issued a warrant to Colonel Edmund Fanning to raise a 500-man battalion of Provincials. Fanning was born on Long Island, New York in 1739, and studied law at Yale before moving to Hillsborough, North Carolina, where he was called to the bar. Noted for his polished manners, obvious intelligence and political cunning, Fanning became one of Governor William Tryon's most trusted representatives. He was deeply involved in frustrating the demands of the poor backcountry settlers of North Carolina, known as the "Regulators," which earned him their hatred. When Tryon was appointed governor of New York, Fanning followed him there. On the outbreak of the rebellion, Tryon was appointed major-general and commander-in-chief of the Provincial Forces in America. Fanning received his warrant with Tryon's patronage.

To assist in raising his regiment, Fanning received financial support of £3,000 from Loyalist subscribers in New York City, Staten Island, King's County, and the town of Jamaica on Long Island. Within a week, he had established his headquarters at Flat Bush on

Long Island, had selected James Grant, an experienced and respected officer, as his major, and was forming the first two companies. Lieutenant-Colonel George Campbell soon joined the regiment, having been selected by Howe without the knowledge or concurrence of Fanning. Fanning resented this interference, and it caused friction among the regimental officers for years to come. In April, 1777, the unit, quartered at Jamaica on Long Island and consisting of six companies, received the title of King's American Regiment. In May, 1777, Fanning's troops were placed on operational status and employed as part of the New York garrison. A month later they were stationed at the strategically important Kingsbridge at the north end of Manhattan Island, under the command of Tryon. In July, 1777, the King's American Regiment had a strength of thirty sergeants, ten drummers, and 420 rank and file, and Inspector General Innes reported that it was in a "very excellent state." Within the year the unit reached its maximum strength of 517 men.

The King's American Regiment remained on active service throughout the war and was widely recognized as an efficient and effective corps. It was involved in a number of incursions into the Hudson River Valley and played a supporting role in the assaults on Forts Montgomery and Clinton. Fanning's unit reinforced the Rhode Island garrison during a combined French and rebel invasion and fought with courage at the siege of Newport and the battle of Quaker Hill. They accompanied Tryon on his raid along the Connecticut coast, landing at New Haven, Fairfield, and Norwalk and participated in General Leslie's expedition to Virginia. Sent to South Carolina, they garrisoned Georgetown and fought the rebels led by Francis Marion and Lieutenant-Colonel "Light Horse" Henry Lee. They reinforced the garrison at Camden and fought at the battle of Hobkirk's Hill; Francis Lord Rawdon commended them for behaving superbly under fire, despite suffering forty-three casualties. After evacuating

Camden and withdrawing back to Charleston, the King's American Regiment was sent to reinforce the British forces in Georgia, where they became part of the Savannah garrison and participated in the struggle to maintain control of the neighbouring districts. The regiment returned to Charleston before sailing to New York. In recognition of their service, they were placed on the American establishment as the 4th American Regiment and later placed on the British establishment. This official recognition enhanced the regiment's prestige, but more importantly, it ensured that the commissioned officers would receive half pay following the termination of hostilities.

A return, dated September, 1783, shows that twenty officers, 128 men, thirty-five women, eighty children, and sixteen servants embarked for the St. John River Valley, while seven other people were already in Nova Scotia. The regiment was disbanded on October 24, 1783, and allocated block six in the parish of Canterbury. Many of the regiment travelled up the St. John River at once and spent a wretched winter at Ste. Anne's Point (now called Fredericton). Not until the following spring did these ex-soldiers reach their land grants in Canterbury. A total of some 300 people associated with the regiment settled in the area, including a group led by Captain Isaac Attwood, that established a community called "Bel-viso," forty miles above Fredericton. Fanning was appointed lieutenant-governor of Nova Scotia in 1783 and lieutenant-governor of Prince Edward Island in 1787.

King's Orange Rangers

The King's Orange Rangers, raised in December, 1776, was one of the first provincial corps. Lieutenant-Colonel John Bayard, a member of an old Hudson River Valley family, recruited soldiers mainly from Orange

County, New Jersey, and Dutchess County, New York. Two of Bayard's sons served in the regiment, and Major Samuel Vetch Bayard became the second in command. Originally organized as a mounted rifle company, the regiment was complete by early 1777, having formed ten companies and recruited 600 men. In July, 1777, it was stationed at Kingsbridge, as part of the New York garrison.

There are conflicting reports on the effectiveness of the Rangers. In a report dated April, 1778, Inspector General Innes notes that "the wretched situation in which the Orange Rangers at present are (one company commanded by Capt Rotton excepted) there is every appearance of neglect and inattention in every part of duty." There must have been a radical improvement, because five months later Muster Master General Winslow observes that "there is not a provincial corps in his Majesty's service, more capable of distinguishing itself, by performance of military exercises than this, nor is there a better body of men." In any event, the Rangers were soon in action.

The Rangers, along with the British 57th Regiment, undertook a successful diversion up the Hudson River in support of Tryon's Danbury Raid. In September, 1777, the regiment joined a raid into New Jersey, marching from Paulus Hook to near Newark. In October, 1777, it participated in Clinton's move up the Hudson River and secured Verplanck's Point during the assaults on Forts Montgomery and Clinton. Once the river was opened up, it accompanied General Sir John Vaughan's forces to within forty-five miles of Albany, in a belated bid to relieve Burgoyne, then trapped at Saratoga. There the Rangers helped raze the towns of Espus and Haverstraw.

In March, 1778, Lieutenant-Colonel Bayard was charged with murdering one of his officers, Lieutenant William Bird, during a heated argument that followed an evening of dining and drinking. A court martial found Bayard guilty of voluntary manslaughter and sentenced him to be cashiered. A review, however, commuted Bayard's sentence to a three-month suspension. Even this lenient sentence was eventually dismissed by King George III on the legal point that having been charged with murder and found not guilty, Bayard could not be sentenced on the charge of manslaughter. During Bayard's suspension, the regiment, with a strength of 208 men, was ordered to reinforce the Halifax garrison.

The Rangers remained in Nova Scotia for the remainder of the war. In addition to being part of the Halifax garrison, they provided detachments for Fort Hughes in the township of Cornwallis and for the protection of the town of Liverpool. Disbanded on Georges Island in Halifax Harbour on October 10, 1783, the King's Orange Rangers was allocated block number fifteen, consisting of a total of 14,250 acres in the parish of St. Martins on the Bay of Fundy. Captain Abraham Van Buskirk and seventy-nine Rangers were given grants, but it is not clear how many actually claimed their land.

Loyal American Regiment

The Loyal American Regiment was raised in New York City in December, 1776, by Colonel Beverley Robinson, Sr., primarily from among the tenants of his large New York estate. The Robinson family home still stands at the foot of Sugar Loaf Mountain overlooking the Hudson River opposite West Point. Born in Virginia, Robinson had served under Wolfe at Quebec and was a dedicated supporter of the King. After Major John André was executed by the rebels for his involvement in the defection of Benedict Arnold, Robinson replaced him as head of the British intelligence service for the remainder of the war. His son, Captain Beverley Robinson, Jr., was subsequently promoted to lieutenant-colonel and replaced his father as regimental commander. Three other sons and a nephew served in the regiment.

The regiment was part of the garrison on Staten Island, played a prominent role in the assaults on Forts Montgomery and Clinton, as well as participating in raids into New Jersey. In June, 1781, it raided Pleasant Valley, New Jersey, in search of cattle and sheep. Although it was continuously engaged by rebel militia, the regiment suffered no casualties and successfully retired with its captured livestock. A return of provincial corps in New York and its outpost, dated August, 1781, shows the regiment with a strength of 236 men, sixty-six women and 127 children. In September, 1781, the unit accompanied Arnold on his raid along the Connecticut coast, where one man was killed and two wounded in the sacking of New London. For the remainder of the war the regiment formed part of the garrison on Long Island.

In October, 1783, 117 officers and men, thirty-nine women, eighty-nine children, and eighteen servants from the Loyal American Regiment embarked for the St. John River Valley. They were allocated block number twelve in the parish of Simonds. Colonel Beverley Robinson, Sr., however, sought refuge in England with "the female part of his family," and Lieutenant-Colonel Beverley Robinson, Jr., settled in Nashwaaksis, opposite Fredericton. He was appointed to the Legislative Council of New Brunswick and given command of the King's New Brunswick Regiment, the provincial corps raised in 1793.

Maryland Loyalists

In September, 1777, during the British occupation of Philadelphia, Sir William Howe approved the establishment of the 1st Battalion of the Maryland Loyalists under the command of Lieutenant-Colonel

James Chalmers. A prominent and outspoken Maryland planter, Chalmers was the author of a pamphlet entitled the *Plain Truth*, rebutting rebel Thomas Paine's well known *Common Sense*. When Philadelphia was evacuated, the Maryland Loyalists moved with the British Army to New York and became part of the garrison on Long Island. The entry of France into the conflict raised concerns about the defence of the British West Indies, so the Maryland Loyalists were dispatched to Jamaica as reinforcements. Duty in Jamaica proved disastrous, the climate and sickness taking a heavy toll on the regiment. With Spain about to enter the war, in January, 1779, the Marylanders were sent to Pensacola in West Florida. At the time they consisted of six companies with a strength of 257 men. When the Spanish governor of Louisiana, Bernardo de Galvez, captured Mobile, his prisoners included a sergeant and fifteen men from the regiment. During the siege of Pensacola, Major Francis Kearney led a daring assault, capturing a Spanish stronghold, destroying seven cannons and inflicting forty casualties on the Spaniards. In recognition of their bravery, Kearney and his Marylanders took charge of a key advanced post. Their courage was again tested when a Spanish shell detonated a powder magazine, demolishing the post and inflicting severe casualties. The Spanish eventually forced the British to capitulate, and the entire garrison, including the Maryland Loyalists, were sent as prisoners to Havana, Cuba. After being paroled, the Marylanders sailed for New York.

In September, 1783, a total of eleven officers, seventy-three soldiers, twelve women, twelve children, and fourteen servants sailed on the transport *Martha* to the St. John River Valley to be disbanded. Tragedy befell the *Martha* when it struck some rocks off Cape Sable. Of 174 the passengers aboard, only thirty-two men, two women, and one child survived. One of the female survivors was pregnant with triplets. Elizabeth Woodward clung to the wreck for three days with her child in her arms, until she and her soldier husband were rescued by fishermen. Soon afterwards she delivered three sons. The surviving Maryland Loyalists, about fifty strong, were assigned block number one in the parish of St. Mary's.

New Jersey Volunteers

The New Jersey Volunteers raised by Brigadier-General Courtland Skinner, the Attorney General of New Jersey, was the largest of the Loyalist provincial corps. Although formed in New York City, its manpower came mainly from New Jersey, particularly from Monmouth and Sussex counties. At its peak the regiment boasted six battalions with a total strength of 2,450 men. Initially overstaffed in officers, the New Jersey Volunteers suffered from high attrition and poor discipline. For a time it was employed in collecting cattle and forage from the surrounding rebel countryside and was derisively dubbed "Skinner's Cowboys" or "Skinner's Greens." Once reorganized and reduced to a more manageable three battalions, the regiment became an effective and reliable unit.

The 1st Battalion served under three commanding officers; Lieutenant-Colonels Elisha Lawrence, Joseph Barton, and Stephen DeLancey. In August, 1777, when part of the Staten Island garrison, Colonel Lawrence and half his battalion were captured after a fierce fight during a rebel dawn attack. In October, 1778, the 1st Battalion with a strength of 354 men embarked for St. Augustine, East Florida to participate in operations in Georgia and South Carolina. By November, 1781, it was back on Long Island as part of the New York garrison. In September, 1783, a total of 232 officers, men, women, children, and servants, travelled to the St. John River Valley, where

The folding campaign chair used by Lieutenant-Colonel Isaac Allen during the American Revolutionary War. NBM

another thirty-eight were already waiting. The 1st Battalion was allocated block number thirteen in the parish of Peel.

The 2nd Battalion was raised in early 1776 by Lieutenant-Colonel John Morris and participated in the Philadelphia Campaign of 1777. After the British Army evacuated Philadelphia, the battalion joined the New York garrison. A muster in May, 1779, records that of the 408 men enlisted in the battalion, 113 had died, seventy-eight had deserted, four had been discharged, and three had transferred to the navy. This left an effective strength of 210 rank and file. The 2nd Battalion participated in the Southern Campaign and returned to New York in January, 1782. It embarked for the St. John River Valley in September, 1783, with a total of 205 officers, men, women, children, and servants. (Twenty-one others were already located in Nova Scotia.) They were allocated block number two in the parish of Kingsclear.

At the time of the surprise dawn attack on Staten Island in August, 1777, the 3rd Battalion was commanded by Lieutenant-Colonel Edward Vaughan Dongan, a young lawyer from Elizabethtown, New Jersey. In the pursuit that followed, Dongan led an assault on the withdrawing rebels and was mortally wounded. Later Lieutenant-Colonel Isaac Allen took command. In October, 1778, the battalion sailed for St. Augustine, East Florida, with a strength of 379 men, to participate in the Southern Campaign in Georgia and South Carolina. Under the command of General Augustine Prevost, Allen's men marched from St. Augustine to capture Savannah, Georgia, and successfully helped defend the city against a combined French and rebel army. In 1780, they served in Augusta, Georgia, and in the spring of 1781, they stoically withstood the twenty-eight-day siege of Fort Ninety-Six in South Carolina. They also participated in the battle of Eutaw Springs. Upon returning to New York, the 3rd Battalion took part in Benedict Arnold's raid on the Connecticut coast against New London and Groton. In September, 1783, a total of 356 officers, men, women, children, and servants embarked for the St. John River Valley. They were allocated block number fourteen in the parish of Wicklow.

New York Volunteers (3rd American Regiment)

Embodied in early 1775 and formally approved in Halifax in January, 1776, the New York Volunteers was one of the first provincial corps to be established. It was initially led by a succession of commanding officers, but in October, 1777, Lieutenant-Colonel George Turnbull took command and retained it until war's end. The regiment was part of the British force that invaded New York in July, 1776, and saw action in the battle of Long Island. At that time it consisted of only two companies; however, it was soon up to strength, properly equipped, and trained. The New York Volunteers campaigned actively for the duration of the war, participating in raids around New York City and into New Jersey. In October, 1778, the regiment, with a strength of 318 men, sailed to East Florida where it assisted in the capture of Savannah and helped defend that city from a combined French and rebel assault. It was the third provincial corps honoured by being placed on the American establishment.

The Volunteers marched overland to join Clinton's successful assault on Charleston. At the battle of Hobkirk's Hill, where the British defeated a superior rebel force, the regiment recorded one man killed, twelve wounded, and fifteen missing, and it launched the battle of Eutaw Springs. Before returning to New York, it was once again stationed at Savannah. In September, 1783, a total of 136 officers, men, women, children, and servants embarked for the St. John River Valley. They were allocated block number three in the parishes of Bright and Queensbury, together with the Guides and Pioneers.

Pennsylvania Loyalists

The history of the 1st Battalion of the Pennsylvania Loyalists mirrors that of the Maryland Loyalists. Following the occupation of Philadelphia, Sir William Howe authorized Lieutenant-Colonel William Allen, Jr. to raise a regiment of provincial corps. Allen had been the commanding officer of the rebel 2nd Pennsylvania Regiment, and had participated in the Quebec campaign, but upon hearing of the Declaration of Independence, he resigned and joined the British Army. The Pennsylvania Loyalists formed part of the Philadelphia garrison and was employed in foraging expeditions across the Delaware River into New Jersey. When the British Army evacuated Philadelphia, it became part of the New York garrison manning outposts on Long Island. In September, 1778, the Pennsylvanians sailed to Halifax with the Maryland Loyalists and then, in December, to Jamaica. In January, 1779, this 165-man battalion, together with the Marylanders, reinforced Pensacola. The following year, in March, it joined German mercenaries to relieve Mobile, then under siege by the Spanish. After an arduous 120-mile march through uninhabited wilderness, it arrived to find Mobile had already surrendered. As the strength of both the Pennsylvania and Maryland Loyalists was seriously depleted, the commander of the Pensacola garrison directed that the two units be combined under the command of Lieutenant-Colonel Allen. Throughout most of the siege of Pensacola, the two units operated as one; however, permission to combine was denied and the Pennsylvania and Maryland Loyalists functioned independently for the remainder of the war. After the capitulation of Pensacola, the Pennsylvania Loyalists was held prisoner in Havana, Cuba, until paroled back to New York. On September 6, 1783, ten officers, forty-one soldiers, twelve women, eleven children, and six servants — a total of eighty people — sailed to the St. John River Valley to be disbanded. They were allocated block number seven in the parish of Southampton.

Prince of Wales American Regiment

Sir William Howe issued a warrant to Montford Browne to raise the Prince of Wales American Regiment in October, 1776, and appointed him colonel. Soon afterwards the ambitious Browne was promoted to the rank of brigadier-general. He hoped that his unit eventually would consist of several battalions, similar to DeLancey's Brigade, but this was not to be. Montford Browne had been the British governor of the Bahamas, but he was carried off by the Continental Navy during a raid on New Providence. While a prisoner in Connecticut, Browne conferred with local Loyalists and developed the concept for his provincial corps. After he was exchanged, he began to recruit with vigour in New York. By April, 1777, the new regiment was at full strength with ten companies, all properly staffed and organized. Howe, without consulting Browne, commissioned Cornet Thomas Pattinson of the 17th Light Dragoons as the lieutenant-colonel; the appointment of this junior regular officer to the command of a provincial corps was not well received.

In May, 1777, some 300 men from the Prince of Wales American Regiment joined Tryon's raid on Danbury, Connecticut. The inclusion of this provincial corps made good sense, as many of the men were from Connecticut. The raiders marched twenty-six miles into enemy territory, destroyed a rebel stores depot, captured fifty-three prisoners and fought a successful withdrawal action back to their waiting ships. Seven men were killed, seventeen wounded, and three discovered missing, with Browne among the wounded. The generals and the local press expressed high praise for the conduct of the regiment in its first major action.

Browne's unit formed part of the New York garrison until being sent as reinforcements to Newport, Rhode Island, where they participated in its successful defence against the combined French and rebel force. The regiment had embarked for Newport with a strength of 443 officers, men, women, and servants, but, fourteen months later, it could muster only 255 men fit for duty. Over this period, though it saw only limited action, the regiment lost 200 men to death, discharge or desertion. When the British evacuated Rhode Island, the remaining members returned to New York.

In April, 1780, the regiment sailed to participate in the Southern Campaign. After the fall of Charleston, it moved to Camden; from there it advanced to Hanging Rock, as part of a force to "awe the disaffected." In the desperate fighting that followed a surprise attack by rebel General Thomas Sumter, the regiment played a decisive role, but at a terrible cost. Ninety-three out of the 181 men involved in the battle became casualties. This loss was among the highest suffered in a single action by any provincial corps during the war, and the Prince of Wales American Regiment did not fully recover.

After the battle of Hanging Rock, the regiment withdrew to Camden but was never again deployed as a unit. Broken into detachments and employed in widely scattered locations, the unit finally sailed back to New York in December, 1782. Lieutenant-Colonel Pattinson requested leave to return to England due to poor health and was replaced by Lieutenant-Colonel Gabriel DeVeber, an experienced provincial officer. In September, 1783, a total of 173 officers and men, sixty-eight women, sixty-one children, and twenty-eight servants left for the St. John River Valley. On October 10, 1783, the Prince of Wales American Regiment was disbanded and allocated block number eleven in the parish of Brighton. Few were satisfied with this remote location, however, and by 1785 only 261 settlers connected with the regiment were located in Brighton. Most went elsewhere, including a group that settled along the Keswick River. DeVeber, concerned about educating his large family, decided to settle closer to Saint John and took up land in nearby Musquash. The community he established is named Prince of Wales.

Queen's Rangers (1st American Regiment)

The Queen's Rangers are among the most famous of the provincial corps. In August, 1776, Howe authorized Robert Rogers, a contro- versial American hero of the Seven Years War, to raise a battalion of rangers. Lieutenant-Colonel Rogers quickly recruited 500 Loyalists, a significant percentage coming from New York and Connecticut, for what was hoped would be a reincarnation of his old corps. Later, the Rangers received reinforcements from independent Loyalist com- panies and rebel deserters. In its first major engagement in October, 1776, it was caught off guard by a rebel night attack at Heathcote Hill, near Mamaroneck, New York. Rogers was rumoured to have mismanaged his corps. He was said to be careless with funds and unscrupulous in recruiting. Early in 1777, Rogers either resigned or was removed from command. Under a series of strong and ex- perienced commanders, the Queen's Rangers was moulded into a disciplined and very effective light infantry regiment.

As part of the New York garrison, the Rangers kept the Con- necticut coast in a state of alarm through a series of raids. They captured the celebrated rebel spy Nathan Hale and fought in the Philadelphia campaign, featuring prominently in the battles of

Brandywine and Germantown. At Brandywine, the Rangers were praised "for their repeated and gallant conduct," but it was here that the regiment suffered its heaviest casualties of the war. Seventy-two officers and men were killed or wounded.

In October, 1777, Captain John Graves Simcoe took command of the Rangers with the provincial rank of major; within nine months, he was promoted to lieutenant-colonel. Simcoe was a dashing young British regular officer and a charismatic leader who had commanded the grenadier company of the 40th Regiment at the battle of Brandywine. He reorganized the Rangers into a mixed force of infantry and cavalry, which briefly also included two small cannons, making it a very powerful and versatile military force.

Under Simcoe, the Rangers mounted a number of daring raids, including the 1778 raids in New Jersey to Quinton's Bridge and Hancock's Bridge. The next year Simcoe led his men sixty miles through rebel country to Von Veghten's Bridge, where they destroyed eighteen flatboats on carriages that Washington urgently needed to cross his army over the Hudson River. In recognition of its effectiveness, the regiment became the first provincial corps to be placed on the American establishment.

The Rangers went on to further acclaim in the Southern Campaign, playing a major role in the capture of Charleston, as well as participating in Benedict Arnold's expedition to Virginia and serving under Cornwallis. Although they were one of the units that capitulated at Yorktown, the Rangers proudly refused to relinquish their regimental colours, hiding them and secretly retrieving them later. A return dated October, 1783, shows a total strength of 344 officers, men, women, children, and servants embarked for the St. John River Valley, with another seven men already waiting in Nova Scotia. The Queen's Rangers was allocated block number five in the parish of Queensbury.

A private soldier of the Royal Fencible Americans, as depicted in Illustration of Uniforms of Loyalist Regiments of the American War of Independence. NBM

Royal Fencible Americans

In March, 1775, General Thomas Gage authorized the raising of the Royal Fencible Americans under the command of Lieutenant-Colonel Joseph Goreham. Although born in Massachusetts, Goreham had settled in Nova Scotia as a young man, beginning his military career in 1744, as a lieutenant in his brother's ranger company. During the Seven Years War he served at the siege of Louisbourg and the capture of Quebec. A major at the siege of Havana, Cuba, he was promoted lieutenant-colonel in 1772. Goreham's first-hand knowledge of Nova Scotia convinced Gage that he and his corps were right for the defence of that colony.

Recruiting began in Massachusetts, and in November, 1775, the regiment was described as consisting mainly "of Europeans and deserters from Whig riflemen," but the composition of the Fencibles changed once they were established in Nova Scotia and recruiting was undertaken locally. Goreham claimed that he had levied "upwards of 500 men" for his regiment.

In June, 1775, Goreham's second in command, Captain Thomas Batt, another experienced officer, sailed to Halifax with an advance party, and he set about aggressively recruiting in what are now Prince Edward Island and Newfoundland. Goreham arrived in Halifax soon afterwards with 100 recruits, and by November the Fencibles had enlisted 390 men. The regiment performed a variety of garrison duties, including fishing to feed the Halifax garrison. In May, 1776, Goreham was appointed commander of Fort Cumberland with a garrison of six companies from the regiment. Although still untrained, the Fencibles under Goreham's command successfully defended the fort against the rebel attack under Jonathan Eddy in 1776.

The Fencibles were stationed in Nova Scotia for the remainder of the war. Brigade Major Gilfred Studholme participated in operations along the St. John River with a fifty-man detachment from this unit, then built and garrisoned Fort Howe at the mouth of the river. The regiment also provided assistance to the navy. In 1778, for example, Lieutenant Constant Connor commanded a detachment, employed as marines, on board the armed schooner *Buckram*. In 1780, Goreham and his men left Fort Cumberland to reinforce the Halifax garrison. The Fencibles built and garrisoned Fort Hughes at the mouth of the Oromocto River in 1781, and a detachment garrisoned Lunenburg. In October, 1782, the strength of the regiment in Nova Scotia totalled twenty-one officers and 239 other ranks.

The Royal Fencible Americans was disbanded at Fort Cumberland and Fort Howe on October 10, 1783, though it remained on ration strength and under military discipline for another fourteen days. Studholme, the commander of Fort Howe, was appointed the agent or commissary to superintend the settlement of Loyalists in the St. John River Valley. The Fencibles were allocated block sixteen consisting of 10,150 acres in the parish of St. George on Passamaquoddy Bay, between Letang and the Magaguadavic River. Captains Peter Clinch and Philip Bailey were entrusted with locating the men on the land, and in November, 1784, a muster shows that 108 men, forty women, and fifty-four children from the regiment had arrived in the district. The Fencibles also received a grant along the Strait of Northumberland, near Port Howe, Nova Scotia.

Royal Highland Emigrants (84th Regiment of Foot)

Lieutenant-Colonel Allan Maclean of Torloisk on the Island of Mull in Scotland, was a pardoned Jacobite and a veteran of the Seven Years War. He presented a memorial to the Secretary of State in London, offering to raise a regiment of Highlanders. On April 3, 1775, King George III approved the formation of a provincial corps to be called the Royal Highland Emigrants and directed the commander-in-chief and the governors of British North America to give Maclean every assistance in raising his regiment. Maclean's mandate was to recruit former Highland soldiers who had settled in North America, as well as recent Highland emigrants. Concurrently, General Thomas Gage in Boston had endorsed a similar proposal presented by Captain John Small. When Maclean arrived in Boston with his royal warrant, Gage readily added his endorsement and to avoid a dispute, directed that the regiment have two battalions.

The largest concentrations of Highland emigrants lived in the Cape Fear region of North Carolina and the Mohawk Valley of New York, and that was where the initial recruiting effort was focused. Each recruit was promised 200 acres free of quit rent for twenty years, forty acres for a wife and each child, and "one Guinea levy-money." The 1st Battalion, under the energetic and demanding leadership of Maclean, was formed in Quebec. It played a crucial role in the siege of Quebec City and in the defence of that province.

Small received a major's commission to raise and command the 2nd Battalion to be established in Nova Scotia. He was a Scot from Perthshire and a veteran of the Seven Years War who had settled in America and was a member of Gage's staff. With the assistance of an old friend, Captain Alexander MacDonald, they began recruiting with determination. They received permission to stop emigrant ships on their way to North America in order to induce the passengers to enlist. It was a controversial gambit but an effective one. When the emigrant ship *Glasgow* was intercepted outside New York City and redirected to Boston, Small interrogated the emigrants and inveigled 100 of them to enlist. MacDonald and Lieutenant Samuel Bliss were despatched from Boston to Halifax in June, 1775, with the task of completing and training the battalion. This was a formidable task, as they lacked experienced officers — not to mention suitable accom-modation, uniforms, equipment, supplies, and arms. They were also thwarted at every step by Governor Francis Legge of Nova Scotia, who was busy attempting to raise his own provincial corps. Mac-Donald, however, was determined, and he persevered.

Since a number of Highlanders had settled on Isle St. John (now called Prince Edward Island) this was deemed a good source of Highland recruits. Ronald McKinnon, an Islander and ex-ensign,

A miniature watercolour of Ensign Alexander MacLean (c. 1779). MacLean was commissioned into the Royal Highland Emigrants in December, 1776. KLHS

was commissioned as a captain and he attracted a number of Island men to join. Other recruits were found in Nova Scotia, and Small forwarded more from Boston. Recruiting parties were also successful in Newfoundland. By December, 1775, the 2nd Battalion, quartered in the Red Barracks in Halifax, consisted of 200 men, organized into five companies, and a year later the battalion was able to claim an establishment of ten companies. On April 1, 1779, the Royal Highland Emigrants, with its two battalions' combined strength of 1,050 men, was placed on the British establishment as a regular regiment, entitled the 84th Regiment of Foot.

The 2nd Battalion was employed in the defence of the Atlantic Provinces. At various times companies and detachments could be found in Halifax, Fort Sackville outside Halifax, Fort Cumberland on the Bay of Fundy, Fort Edward at Windsor, Fort Anne at Annapolis Royal, Fort Hughes in the Township of Cornwallis, Fort Howe on the St. John River, in and around St. John's and Placentia in Newfoundland, and in Sydney on Cape Breton protecting the coal mines. In October, 1780, Small and five companies of the 2nd Battalion joined Leslie's expedition to Virginia and later campaigned in South Carolina. Two of these companies were employed on garrison duty in Charleston and then sent as reinforcements to Jamaica, while the other three companies were placed under Lord Rawdon's command. Although this detachment of the 84th Regiment lost its separate identity, it helped relieve Fort Ninety-Six and fought at the battles of Hobkirk's Hill and Eutaw Springs. In November, 1782, after the evacuation of Charleston, the detachment returned to Halifax.

The majority of the 2nd Battalion members were disbanded on October 10, 1783. Those wishing to remain in North America were demobilized at Windsor and those wishing to return to Britain, in Halifax. A tract of land was granted to Small's battalion in the township of Douglas, Hants County, near Windsor, but some soldiers opted to go elsewhere, including a group that settled near Lake Utopia, outside St. George, New Brunswick.

Westchester Refugees

The Westchester Refugees was such an effective operational unit that it is frequently identified as a provincial corps; however, it was a militia regiment. When the British regained control of New York in October, 1776, four prominent Loyalists from Westchester County, New York, were commissioned to raise independent militia companies. The original intent was to use these troops to assist the British authorities in regaining civil control, but they soon became involved in harassing and raiding rebel positions. During the winter of 1776-1777, the four companies were combined and called the Westchester Militia. Further reorganizations occurred, and by the end of 1779, Lieutenant-Colonel

A mounted soldier of the Westchester Refugees (1780), as depicted in Illustration of Uniforms of Loyalist Regiments of the American War of Independence. NBM

James Delancey was appointed commander of the 500-man unit with the title of Westchester Refugees. Delancey retained command until the regiment was disbanded.

The Westchester Refugees was tasked to maintain control of the southern part of Westchester County; to dominate the area between the rebel and British lines; and to obtain intelligence and provide horses, forage, and supplies to the New York garrison. Delancey established his headquarters and a secure encampment for displaced Loyalists at Morrisania, a location in southern Westchester County, which provided easy access to rebel territory and a protected crossing site over the Harlem River to Manhattan Island. With seizing cattle being a prime pursuit, the unit earned the nickname "Delancey's Cowboys"; Delancey claimed that one third of the meat supplied to the British Army was obtained by the Westchester Refugees.

The partisan war the Westchester Refugees waged was a particularly bitter one. A struggle between neighbours, and frequently be tween family members, it was marked by sudden alarms, terrifying raids, and deadly ambushes over familiar ground. Atrocities were not unknown, but James Delancey was a respected officer with a reputation for exercising command with a firm hand, maintaining rigid discipline, and operating within the accepted laws of war.

The exploits of the Westchester Refugees were many. In the spring of 1781, for example, Delancey received detailed intelligence concerning the location of the headquarters of the rebel 1st Rhode Island Regiment at Davenport House near the Croton River. With a force of 260 men, he led a raid to capture the rebels' commanding officer, Colonel Christopher Greene. The Refugees travelled through the night, waiting just short of the Croton River until dawn, when Delancey's spies suggested that the rebel night guard would be withdrawn. They then forded the river and caught Greene's headquarters totally by surprise. The rebels surrendered, but then, for some unexplained reason, a young officer suddenly fired from an upstairs window. The volley was promptly returned and the building stormed. Two rebel officers and twelve others were killed, and about ten wounded. Thirty were taken prisoner, including the mortally wounded Greene. The only Refugee casualty was Lieutenant Gilbert Totten, who received a minor wound.

Sir Guy Carleton, who was responsible for orchestrating the British exodus from New York, had well founded concerns about protecting the Loyalists of Westchester County and the Refugees from acts of revenge and violence. He ensured that precautions were taken to provide them a safe withdrawal and asylum. On June 5, 1783, a total of 493 Westchester Refugees and their families left New York on board the Brig HMS *Thesis* and the transport ship *Nicholas and Jane*, bound for Fort Cumberland on the Bay of Fundy. On July 15, the ships dropped anchor and the passengers set up a tented camp outside the walls of Fort Cumberland. To the Refugees' disappointment, there was a delay in making the necessary arrangements, but eventually two grants were designated for the Refugees; one on the Strait of Northumberland, west of the village of Tatamagouche, and the second along the military road that ran between Halifax and Fort Cumberland. The commissary at Fort Cumberland provided transportation to assist the soldiers and their families move to their grants. By September, however, more than half of the Refugees remained at Fort Cumberland. Many of these opted to settle in Westmorland County or in the city of Saint John where some of their descendants still live.

CHAPTER FOUR

The Legacy of the Military Loyalists

The Provincials Take Root in New Brunswick

Although Sir Guy Carleton was extremely sympathetic to the plight of the Loyalists, he faced major difficulties. Authorities in London had directed him to merely transport the provincial corps to Halifax and to disband them immediately upon arrival. Carleton knew this was unacceptable. He arranged to have the regiments disbanded nearer to their proposed land grants, and he delayed the dates of discharge to provide time to adjust. At Carleton's urging, the Treasury Board extended the issue of food rations for one year after the provincial corps were disbanded, two-thirds ration allowance in the second year, and one-third in the year three. It was hoped that the Loyalists could clear their land, make it productive, and be self-sufficient within three years.

The Crown also supplied each refugee with basic essentials, such as tools, cloth, shoes, and stockings. In addition, each family was given one good blanket and each single man a damaged one. The British government approved a grant of ten million pounds for relief. The St. John River refugees received their portion of this fund mainly in building supplies. In a twelve-month period nearly two million feet of boards, a million and a half of shingles, and 7,500 clapboards were issued. Still the Loyalists faced an uncertain future.

Once the Loyalists had arrived in the Maritimes, the term "Provincial" was used to distinguish those with a military connection from "civilian refugees." In general terms, the bulk of the Provincials were disbanded in New Brunswick and the majority of civilians were landed in Nova Scotia. However, the demarcation between the two groups was never absolute. Some civilians had served in the military earlier in the war; some had sailed with the navy, on merchant ships or with privateers; and some had fought with paramilitary units, such as the "Associated Loyalists." Others had performed support roles with the commissariat, the engineer branch, or the barrack-master general department. Regardless of background, all confronted the same challenge of rebuilding their lives in a wild new land.

The delay in arranging transportation for the Loyalists gave the governor of Nova Scotia, Colonel John Parr, some breathing space. Arrangements were made to survey three unoccupied areas of the province for Loyalist settlement — Port Roseway, renamed Shelburne; the St. John River Valley; and the Passamaquoddy Bay. The first Loyalist fleet from New York arrived in the spring of 1783 and was directed to Shelburne and the St. John River Valley. Towns sprang up over night, overwhelming the local military commissioners who had the responsibility for establishing these new settlements and providing essential support. On May 11, a fleet of twenty transports sailed around Partridge Island, and after a thunderous welcome from

Fort Howe's cannon, dropped anchor in Saint John Harbour. For seven interminably long days, the passengers waited for final preparations to be completed. The Loyalist families had been crammed on board the transport ships for a month before they were finally allowed to disembark at what is now Market Slip in the city of Saint John. They were warmly received by the commander of Fort Howe, Brigade Major Gilfred Studholme, who did everything possible to help. Only the transport *Union* did not stop at Saint John. Instead, it sailed directly to the Kingston Peninsula, where its passengers immediately took up their grants of land.

On June 29, the summer fleet arrived in the St. John River with more Loyalists from New York, further taxing available resources and accommodations. This group consisted of 500 men, 335 women, 743 children, and 394 servants for a total of 1,972. Before these refugees could be settled, the fall fleet arrived, disembarking 3,000 more refugees on October 1. Since these were mainly families of provincial corps destined for lands up river, they were encamped above the Reversing Falls. Due to the late season, the shortage of transport, and the uncertainty of land grant locations, most remained there, to spend an uncomfortable and frustrating winter. The last of the transport ships arrived in December. When winter arrived, the population had grown to 5,000, and 1,500 new dwellings had been erected in what became the city of Saint John. The original inhabitants of Portland Point were swallowed up by the newcomers. The bitterly cold weather, inadequate housing, and coarse food resulted in much suffering and death, particularly among the children and the elderly.

Members of the 3rd Battalion of the New Jersey Volunteers and the King's American Regiment experienced even greater hardship. They were determined to reach their land grants without delay, so that they would be in a position to plant as soon as spring arrived. With courage and determination they pushed their way up river to

The entrance to the Old Loyalist Burying Ground, between Brunswick and George streets, Fredericton. DEPARTMENT OF TOURISM, CITY OF FREDERICTON

Ste. Anne's Point, where Fredericton now stands, but before they could erect suitable shelters, winter struck early and with a vengeance. In addition to deplorable living conditions, these Loyalists faced starvation, due to the difficulties of transporting provisions up river. The Loyalist burying ground at Salamanca in Fredericton bears silent witness to their suffering. Despite these and other hardships, the Loyalists persevered. Of the 80,000 to 100,000 refugees eager to flee New York at the end of the American Revolutionary War, 30,000 were evacuated to Nova Scotia, of which some 14,000 settled in what was to become New Brunswick

When the long awaited spring of 1784 arrived, most of the Loyalists were only too glad to leave their miserable winter encampments and set out to claim their land. The regimental blocks of land for the provincial corps were situated along the St. John River, and that is where the majority headed. Another large group, displaced Loyalists from the Penobscot region of Maine, settled in the Passamaquoddy Bay area, mainly at St. Andrews and along the St. Croix River. Other smaller groups selected land along the Petitcodiac River, the Vale of Sussex, Sackville, the Miramichi River, and the Bay of Chaleur. In short order, disbanded soldiers could be found in every corner of New Brunswick, establishing new communities and overwhelming the existing ones. Prior to the arrival of the Loyalists, the total population of the province was only about five thousand. Half were Native and the remainder divided between the Acadians and pre-Loyalists, known as Planters, who settled here after 1763. The sheer weight of numbers meant that the Loyalists instantly became the dominant group.

The concept of settling the various provincial corps in tidy regimental blocks quickly collapsed. Many grants proved unsuitable for farming, and some of the blocks were considered too remote. Friendships and family ties influenced where many people wanted to settle.

Then there were those who were uninterested in farming and sought sites where they could practise their trades or enter business. Some preferred urban life. Sadly, some simply could not make the necessary adjustment or face another challenge, and turned to liquor and other escapes. It must also be recognized that this settlement concept was based on the faulty premise that disbanded soldiers, after years of military service, could be remoulded without difficulty into success-ful, contented farmers. It is estimated that only one in ten actually went to his claim, and not even all of these remained for any period of time. Some caught the "Niagara fever," accepting the offer of free land by John Graves Simcoe, the first lieutenant-governor of Upper Canada and ex-commanding officer of the Queen's Rangers. About fifteen percent left New Brunswick, mainly to move to Upper Canada or to return to the United States. What is amazing is how many Loyalists remained in New Brunswick and built new lives for themselves and their families.

Claiming land grants was merely the first of many difficult steps. Clearing the land and bringing it into production required years of back-breaking labour. An example of success is Benjamin Ingraham and his family. He was a tenant farmer in New Concord in Albany County, New York, when the American Revolutionary War broke out. Ingraham's only interest lay in working his farm and providing for his young family. He had no desire to support the rebel cause, but was soon persecuted for his indifference. Forced to flee, he left his family to face the wrath of their rebel neighbours. In 1776, Ingraham enlisted in the King's American Regiment and was promoted to ser-geant. For seven years, he saw action around New York, in Rhode Island, and in the Southern Campaign. In 1783, in spite of the wrath of vengeful neighbours, he returned to New Concord, collected his family, and emigrated to New Brunswick with his regiment. His twelve-year-old daughter Hannah provides a poignant account of that first miserable winter at Ste. Anne's Point. She recounts how gladly her family abandoned their tent for the new log shack her father built, even though it lacked a floor, chimney, and door. As soon as the family moved, they boiled water, melted butter, and toasted bread for breakfast. Her mother was so thankful for that humble shelter that she offered a prayer: "Thank God we are no longer in dread of having shots fired through our house. This is the sweetest meal I ever tasted for many a day." Ingraham soon learned that the land upon which he had built his first home had been designated for a college, so he petitioned and received a grant further upriver at Bear Island in Lower Queensbury. In time, he became a successful farmer and his many descendants maintain deep roots in the area to this day. It was the perseverance of men like Ingraham and their families that ensured a modest agricultural prosperity for the new colony.

Not all Provincials were equal, however. One in ten Loyalists arriving in Nova Scotia was Black, and some of these had served in provincial corps. As early as April, 1776, General Sir Henry Clinton formed Blacks into pioneer companies. Pioneers were skilled and unskilled labourers who were employed in a variety of tasks to assist military operations. In late 1777 or early 1778, a unit called the Company of Black Pioneers was formally raised in Philadelphia under the command of a white officer, Captain Allen Stewart. This unit saw action in several theatres of war, including the Southern Campaign, and was disbanded in Nova Scotia in 1783. The Loyalist emigration to New Brunswick included about 300 free Blacks and 500 Blacks listed as "servants," which usually meant slaves. No recognition or account was kept of those with military service. The free Blacks were encouraged to form themselves into companies to assist in their settlement. Grants of land were set aside in three areas: Willow Grove near Loch Lomond, Milkish Creek on the Kingston Peninsula, and Elm Tree on the Otnabog Creek south of Gagetown. The land al-

The house at 808 Brunswick Street, Fredericton, was built for the Hon. Jonathan Odell, Chaplain to the King's American Dragoons. He later became a member of the New Brunswick Executive Council. PANB

located to Blacks was poor and they received a grant of only fifty acres each, half that given to white Loyalists. The obstacles confronting these settlers were almost insurmountable, and, not surprisingly, few succeeded as independent farmers.

The Provincials exerted a strong influence on New Brunswick from their arrival. The first lieutenant-governor of the new province was Colonel Thomas Carleton, a professional soldier with a solid military reputation earned on a number of foreign and American postings. He believed that the seat of government should be in a central location, and his reasons for selecting Fredericton included its large population of disbanded soldiers. The presence of Provincials ensured a society in which Carleton would feel comfortable. It is not surprising that Carleton, in attending to governmental affairs, surrounded himself with Provincials, and named the city after King George III's second son, Frederick, a patron of the army. Carleton's executive council consisted of men such as Colonel George D. Ludlow of DeLancey's Brigade; Jonathan Odell, Chaplain to the King's American Dragoons; Lieutenant-Colonel Beverley Robinson, Jr., of the Loyal American Regiment; Major John Coffin of the King's American Regiment; Brigade Major Gilfred Studholme of the Royal Fencible Americans; and Edward Winslow, the former muster master general, and his deputy Ward Chipman. Carleton dispensed other civilian and military appointments, filling them mainly with Provincials; for example, Lieutenant-Colonel Isaac Allen of the New Jersey Volunteers and Major Joshua Upham of the King's American Dragoons were selected as Supreme Court judges. There can be little doubt that the Provincials and their values strongly influenced the evolution of New Brunswick.

As a pre-condition to his appointment as lieutenant-governor, Carleton insisted that he have command of any regular forces in the province, and as commander-in-chief of the militia, he was given a free hand with the local defence force. Although appointments to county militia regiments carried no emoluments, they did reflect the appointee's standing in the community. In his selection of militia colonels, Carleton chose men of prominence, proven loyalty, and military experience. These criteria favoured Provincials. The colonels, in turn, recommended commissioning men they knew and respected, frequently former comrades-in-arms. As a result, the Provincials dominated the newly founded militia. Similarly, when Carleton received authority in 1793 to raise a provincial corps to be called the King's New Brunswick Regiment, the officers were recruited from the ranks of half pay officers with experience in the Revolutionary War;

A miniature believed to be a portrait of Lieutenant-Colonel Isaac Allen of the New Jersey Volunteers. Allen later became a judge of the Supreme Court of New Brunswick. NBM

Lieutenant-Colonel Beverley Robinson, Jr., formerly of the Loyal American Regiment, was appointed its commanding officer. For the next thirty years, whenever there was a war or threat of one, the Provincials and their sons answered the call to arms without hesitation. A strong military tradition developed in the province, one that would continue with the raising of the Fighting 26th Battalion during World War I, and the North Shore Regiment, and the Carleton and York Regiment during World War II.

The Loyalist legacy also contributed to a strong sense of fealty to the British Crown, including an unquestioning belief in the benefits of British culture and traditions, which remained evident throughout the nineteenth and early twentieth centuries. It followed that close imperial ties would protect the colony against the perceived brash materialism and rude republicanism of their American neighbours. New Brunswickers felt pride in their connection with the British Empire, as demonstrated in the province's ready support of Britain during the South African War and the two World Wars. In the modern context, this sense of place and loyalty has been transformed into a strong belief in Canada.

The Provincials' belief in strong leadership, as experienced in the military, left a unique perspective concerning government and community. Although a hierarchical society was never established in New Brunswick, there remained a belief in leadership at the political level and in the ability of government to create a stable and harmonious society. Perhaps as a result of their experience of persecution in the rebellion, the Loyalists stressed the need for a credible legal system and based New Brunswick's on the ancient and tried principles of British Common Law. They imparted a keen sense of order to their new society, giving precedence to the requirement for law and order. Moreover, while still struggling to tame the wilderness, the Loyalists made establishing grammar schools and a college one of their first priorities. This emphasis on the importance of education endures today in New Brunswick's many universities. Having suffered for their dissenting views, the Loyalists brought a deep understanding of the basic need for political, religious, and racial tolerance. It can be said that the Canadian belief in a tolerant and humane society is part of the Loyalist legacy.

Gravestone of Colonel David Fanning of the North Carolina Militia.
JOHN DEMINGS, DIGBY NS

CHAPTER FIVE

People and Places

*Selected New Brunswick Military Loyalist
and Revolutionary War Sites*

New Brunswick owes its origins to the American Revolutionary War, and many traces of the conflict can still be found around the province today, especially through the artifacts, sites and monuments associated with the Loyalists. These vestiges enrich the province's heritage landscape and stand as ongoing reminders of the vital roles the Loyalists played in New Brunswick's historical development.

Fort Cumberland

Fort Beauséjour National Historic Site is located at Aulac, five min-utes north of the Nova Scotia border. The ruins of the old fort occupy a commanding, but bleak, ridge rising a hundred feet above the

Merritt House, also known as the Loyalist House, completed in 1817. It is located at Union and Germain streets, Saint John. HRSJ, CAIRNES 0307

Tantramar Marshes. Fort Beauséjour was built by the French in 1751 and captured by the British in 1755 during the Seven Years War. After improving its fortifications, the British renamed it Fort Cumberland and maintained it as a military post until 1835. This is the fort that Lieutenant-Colonel Joseph Goreham and the Royal Fencible Americans successfully defended against an invading rebel army under Colonel Jonathan Eddy in the autumn of 1776.

Saint John: The Loyalist City

From its founding, Saint John has been one of the most active seaports on the Atlantic coast. It takes great pride in its Loyalist roots and promotes itself as the "Loyalist City." This connection can be found in many sites and symbols. The Loyalists landed at Market Slip and gave the downtown streets clearly Royalist names. The two main streets (King Street and Charlotte Street) and squares (King's Square and Queen's Square) are named for King George III and Queen Charlotte, the reigning monarchs during the American Revolutionary War. Prince William Street is named for their son, who later became William IV; Princess Street for their youngest daughter Princess Amelia; and Saint James Street for one of their London palaces. The Old Loyalist Burying Ground can be found at Sidney and King Streets, with the earliest surviving gravestone, in memory of Conradt Hendricks, dated July 13, 1784. At 120 Union Street is the Georgian style Loyalist House designated a national historical site. It was built between 1817 and 1820 for David Daniel Merritt, a New York Loyalist. His descendants occupied the house for over 150 years, and it is now a museum. Outside flies the Royal Union Flag, proclaimed in 1606, and carried into battle by the provincial corps.

Fort Howe

On the hill off Magazine Street stands a reconstructed blockhouse, marking the site where Fort Howe once commanded the Saint John Harbour. Today, it is a national historic site and provides a breathtaking panoramic view of Saint John.

In order to retain control of the St. John River, Brigade Major Gilfred Studholme was sent in November, 1777 to establish a military post at its entrance. He arrived with fifty men from his regiment, the Royal Fencible Americans, and four 6-pounder cannons. Included in the cargo was a blockhouse; it had been built in Halifax, dismantled, loaded on board, and was ready to be reassembled on arrival. Studholme opted not to build on the site of Fort Frederick, the older British fortification, but to erect his fort on the hill which dominated the harbour. Despite the late season, the soldiers, with the help of the local residents, set to work with resolve and within weeks blockhouse, barracks, and defence works were completed. The fort was named after the British commander-in-chief, General Sir William Howe. Studholme, who was held in high regard for his integrity and judgment, remained in command until his regiment was disbanded in 1783. Although the fort was never attacked, it achieved its purpose of maintaining control over the area and influencing the inhabitants, both Native and white. When the Loyalist refugees arrived in 1783, it was used as a commissary for dispensing food and supplies.

Brigadier-General Benedict Arnold of the American Legion

Although his name is one of the best known from the American Revolution, Benedict Arnold is seldom linked with the Loyalists, despite meeting all the qualifications for that title. Arnold was in London, promoting yet another grand scheme for British victory when the war ended. The British defeat found Arnold and his family spurned socially and rebuffed by those in authority. Disenchanted, he sailed for New Brunswick in October, 1785, in the hope of starting anew. All that first winter, Arnold carefully assessed business opportunities along the St.

A tall-case clock, owned by Brigadier-General Benedict Arnold of the American Legion. KLHS

John River. He opened a lumberyard at Lower Cove in Saint John and staked out 1,000 forested acres in Maugerville as a source of lumber. He also purchased waterfront property on Broad Street for a wharf and warehouse, a lot fronting on Main Street for a general store, and several other town lots on speculation. He selected a gambrel-roofed clapboard house on Broad Street as a home for his growing family. To support his business interests, Arnold bought four lots in Fredericton along Waterloo Row and built a warehouse at its junction with University Avenue. A plaque at 102 Waterloo Row recognizes this connection. Unfortunately, Arnold's combative and aggressive nature resulted in endless legal disputes, animosity with partners, and a failure to win acceptance. After six years, Arnold again became disheartened, sold his assets, auctioned off the contents of his Saint John home, and sailed back to England. One of the items Arnold left behind was his tall-case clock, which can now be seen in the parlour of the Morehouse House at Kings Landing Historical Settlement, north of Fredericton.

Major John Coffin of the King's American Regiment

A grave marker in Woodman's Point cemetery on Highway 102 near Westfield marks the passing of John Coffin, an effective and delightfully rambunctious officer. The third son of Nathaniel Coffin, the last Receiver of His Majesty's Customs in the port of Boston, he came from a prominent New England family. In March, 1778, Coffin was appointed captain in the King's Orange Rangers. He soon found garrison duty dull and exchanged positions with Captain John Howard in order to join the New York Volunteers, a unit earmarked for the Southern Campaign. Coffin was given command of the light infantry company, which he led with acclaim in the capture and defence of Savannah, the capture of Charleston, and the battle of Rocky Mount. His company was converted into a troop of mounted infantry, which he commanded at the battle of Camden, receiving commendation for bravery and a promotion to brevet major. Coffin again distinguished himself at the battle of Eutaw Springs and in a successful independent action at Videau Bridge, Berkeley County, where fifty-seven rebels were killed and twenty wounded at the cost of only one killed and one wounded among the Provincials. He was then transferred to the King's American Regiment to fill a vacant major's position and given command of an advanced post at the Quarter House outside Charleston. When the regiment returned to New York, Coffin's aggressive nature quickly led him into conflict

A silhouette of Major John Coffin of the King's American Regiment, prepared late in his life. KLHS

with his abrasive commanding officer, Lieutenant-Colonel George Campbell. They argued violently and publicly in the street over the employment of a clerk. Coffin demanded a court of inquiry into the affair and when that failed to provide satisfaction, a duel was arranged. Four shots were exchanged. One shot scratched Campbell on the right thigh and a second took a button off his coat. Coffin received a ball in the groin, which was feared to be mortal, but to everyone's surprise, the indestructible Coffin recovered.

While in Charleston, Coffin had found time to court and marry a southern lady named Anne Matthew. When he arrived at Fort Howe with the spring fleet, he brought his wife and four slaves from Charleston. He purchased about 6,000 acres along the Nerepis River, where he built a home which he called "Alwington Manor." He represented King's County in the Provincial Assembly. Again he became involved in an altercation ending in a duel, this time resulting in the wounding of a fellow representative, Captain James Glennie. Coffin had been placed on half pay effective 1783 when he was

A watercolour of John Coffin's house, Alwington Manor, Westfield, by George Neilson Smith (1839). NBM, JOHN CLARENCE WEBSTER CANADIANA COLLECTION, W413.

twenty-seven. He continued to draw his half pay for fifty-five years, and in addition, he received regular promotions, so that when he died, he was one of the most senior generals in the British Army. However, he never mellowed with age or rank. On July 27, 1813, an incredulous British regular officer noted that General Coffin had been fined for selling rum without a licence and could be found "selling cabbages" at the Saint John market. He died at the age of eighty-seven in 1838.

Ensign Henry Nase of the King's American Regiment

The provincially designated historic Mount Hope farmhouse at 690 Nerepis Road in Grand Bay-Westfield was built by Henry Nase in 1786. The property remains in family hands. In April, 1778, Nase enlisted in the King's American Regiment as a private soldier and saw continuous service as part of the New York garrison, on excursions up the Hudson River, and in the battle of Rhode Island. In April, 1780, he was appointed to the position of regimental sergeant major, the highest rank for a non-commissioned soldier. In this capacity, he served in the Southern Campaign and saw action in Virginia, South Carolina, and Georgia. Upon his regiment's return to New York, he was commissioned to the rank of ensign in recognition of his dedicated service. In April, 1783, Ensign Nase sailed with an advance party to Annapolis Royal in Nova Scotia and then on to Saint John to reconnoiter land for members of the regiment. Two years after building his home at Mount Hope, he married Jane Quinton. He went on to become a magistrate, a lieutenant-colonel in the militia, and an active churchman. Henry Nase died in 1836, at the age of eighty-four, and is buried with his wife in the family graveyard near 273 Nerepis Road, Westfield. A beautiful stained-glass memorial window in the local Anglican Church is dedicated to him.

Lieutenant-Colonel Richard Hewlett of DeLancey's Brigade

Richard Hewlett was born in 1729 in Hampstead, Queens County, Long Island, New York. He built his New Brunswick home at a location he also called Hampstead, in Queens County, opposite Long Island in the St. John River. Built in 1785, the home still stands and is considered the oldest documented residence in New Brunswick.

Hewlett was a veteran of the Seven Years War. He raised a company and served as a captain under General James Abercromby at the attack on Fort Ticonderoga on Lake Champlain in New York, and under Colonel John Bradstreet at the capture of Fort Frontenac on Lake Ontario. At the outbreak of the Revolutionary War, Hewlett was an outspoken Loyalist. His views were so strongly held that the governor of New York, William Tryon, entrusted him with the responsibility for securing militia arms and ammunition from the rebels. The Continental Congress listed Hewlett as a traitor who must be imprisoned at all cost, and orders were issued more than once for his arrest. However, Hewlett bravely stood his ground against rebel intimidation.

When DeLancey's Brigade was formed, Hewlett was appointed lieutenant-colonel of the 3rd Battalion. He retained that appointment until the war's end, although when the 1st and 2nd Battalions were combined, his unit was renumbered the 2nd Battalion. He and his battalion remained on Long Island, their most noteworthy action being the defence of Setauket against an attack by Colonel Abraham

Parsons, the commander of the rebel whaleboat privateers. When Parsons made an insolent demand for surrender, Hewlett curtly refused, saying to his men, "I will stand by you as long as there is a man left." Upon the evacuation of New York, General Sir Guy Carleton appointed Hewlett commander of all the provincial corps going to the St. John River Valley. He was responsible for disbanding them, ensuring that they received their allotted supplies, and assisting them to obtain their land grants. Hewett died at the age of fifty-nine in 1789. His prominent grave marker can be found in the St. Stephen's Anglican Church cemetery in Queenstown.

Colonel David Fanning of the North Carolina Militia

Near the village of Hampstead in Queens County, Fanning Brook runs into the St. John River opposite Spoon Island. Behind, in the military training area of CFB Gagetown stands Fanning Mountain. These two geographic features are named for Colonel David Fanning, who owned a 489-acre tract of land containing the brook, upon which he operated a gristmill.

From the very beginning of the Revolutionary War, Fanning was involved in the bitter civil strife that took place in the backcountry of the Carolinas. He had been captured several times by the rebels, but always managed to escape. In October, 1778, Fanning was taken once again, and on this occasion was held in the jail at Fort Ninety-Six in South Carolina. To prevent his escape, the rebels stripped him naked and chained him to the middle of the floor of a thirty-square-foot room, forty-five feet above ground, with four grates open to the winter weather. Unbelievably, after an almost two-month confinement in these appalling conditions, he broke out. In the ensuing pur-

A bayonet, scabbard, and account book owned by Colonel David Fanning of the North Carolina Militia. JOHN DEMINGS, DIGBY NS

suit, with a price on his head, Fanning was wounded twice but made good his escape. In July, 1781, after being elected by its members, he was formally appointed colonel of the Randolph and Chatham County Militia of North Carolina.

Colonel Fanning was the most successful and daring guerrilla commander in North Carolina. He never lost a battle. His most renowned exploit was a raid on Hillsborough, in which he captured the rebel state governor, his council, and 200 prisoners (half of whom were Continental soldiers), at the cost of only one Loyalist wounded. Although his war record had no equal, Fanning was a controversial figure; his egotistical and aggressive character led to endless problems with his neighbours and the authorities in New Brunswick. These difficulties culminated in a charge of rape involving a neighbour's daughter. Fanning was found guilty and sentenced to death, but his wife made a desperate plea for mercy, and the sentence was commuted to exile. He and his family moved to the neighbouring colony of Nova Scotia. Gravestones, in memory of both Fanning and his wife, can be found in the Anglican Church cemetery in Digby.

Fort Hughes

A reconstruction of Fort Hughes stands in Sir Douglas Hazen Park in the town of Oromocto. The Royal Fencible Americans built the original fort in 1781, at the junction of the St. John and Oromocto Rivers, about 150 yards below the old highway bridge. The garrison of the fort consisted of twenty-five men from the Fencibles under the command of Boston-born Lieutenant Constant Connor. Fort Hughes was established for three purposes: to protect the important lumbering operation in the area, to provide a relay station on the vital overland route between Quebec City and Halifax, and to ensure that the neighbouring community of Maugerville did not rediscover its rebel sympathies. The lumbering operation was of strategic importance as it provided the British Royal Navy with much needed masts for its warships. William Davidson, who had abandoned his lumber operation in the Miramichi River Valley because of the predatory rebel privateers, received permission from Governor Hughes of Nova Scotia to cut masts in the St. John River Valley. The value of this vital resource was recognized when the first cargo of masts left for England in November, 1778. After the regiment was disbanded, Lieutenant Connor received and settled on a grant of 700 acres in the area of Oromocto Flats and Thatch Island. In tribute to the garrison, the crest of the town of Oromocto includes the figures of two soldiers of the Fencibles.

Loyalist Encampment and Cemetery

A granite boulder with a plaque is located on the Green opposite Alexandra Street in Fredericton. It honours the Loyalists who founded the city and also marks where the first arrivals spent the miserable winter of 1783-1784 encamped in temporary shelters. Just past the ball diamond, and along the Salamanca walking trail, is a secluded cemetery that is the final resting place of those Loyalists who did not survive the hardship of this winter encampment. It contains a few grave markers, too weathered to read.

Ensign Thomas Gill of the Maryland Loyalists

A stone house of Georgian design fronts the St. John River at 968 Riverside Drive in Lower St. Mary's, York County. This is the home Thomas Gill built for his family in 1788. Gill, a Loyalist from Delaware, served six years with the Maryland Loyalists as a non-commissioned officer. He fought at the siege of Pensacola, Florida, was captured by the Spanish and held prisoner in Cuba. In recognition of his service, he was commissioned ensign in July, 1783.

Gill was aboard the ill-fated transport *Martha* when she was wrecked off Seal Island on her way to the St. John River. The *Martha* struck the rocks before dawn at a location afterwards known as Soldiers' Ledge, and the passengers desperately attempted to keep the vessel afloat by manning the pumps. When this proved futile, the longboat was launched, but it was smashed when the main mast fell overboard. The ship's captain then ordered that the last two vessels on board be launched, a cutter and a jolly boat. Countering all naval tradition, the captain suddenly jumped into the jolly boat, transferred to the cutter, and as the terrified passengers watched, set the empty jolly boat free and sailed off in the cutter. Gill was one of the few to survive this traumatic experience, but his wife and child perished. He married again in Saint John, and then moved up river to take up his grant of 550 acres. He died in St. Mary's in 1833.

Lieutenant Anthony Allaire of the Loyal American Regiment

In the Simonds family plot in the Old Loyalist Burying Ground in Fredericton stands a grave marker with the simple words, "Sacred to the memory of Anthony Allaire, born 22 of Feb 1755, died 9 June 1838." Anthony Allaire was born in New Rochelle in Westchester County, New York. Of Huguenot ancestry, he was for unexplained reasons the only member of his family to remain loyal to the Crown. On April 20, 1777, Allaire was commissioned a lieutenant in the Loyal American Regiment. He served as part of the New York garrison and took part in the storming of the Hudson River strongholds of Forts Montgomery and Clinton. In 1779, Major Patrick Ferguson was seeking provincial volunteers to join his new corps of riflemen, the American Volunteers, for special service in the Carolinas; Allaire was one of those selected.

Allaire was with Ferguson's corps on the march from Savannah to Charleston; he was at the successful night attack at Monck's Corner, the capture of the rebel strong point at Lampries Point, and in operations around Fort Ninety-Six. He survived unscathed the stunning rebel victory at the battle of King's Mountain, though twenty of the seventy members of Ferguson's corps were killed and thirty-three wounded. He witnessed with horror the murder of some 100 surrendered Loyalist militiamen and was present at a kangaroo court a week later, when a further nine Loyalists prisoners were hanged. He eventually escaped from the rebels and returned to complete the war with his original unit, the Loyal American Regiment. Anthony Allaire's diary, which covers his service with Ferguson and the momentous events at King's Mountain, can be found in the New Brunswick Museum in Saint John.

After the war, Allaire married Mary Simonds, and they built a home called "Pine Grove" in the parish of Douglas, across the river from Fredericton on the spot where the York Manor Nursing Home now stands.

Captain John Saunders of the Queen's Rangers

Several sites relate to the prominent Loyalist John Saunders. The modest Fredericton house at 752 King Street was built for him in either 1795 or 1796 as a town residence. Saunders's second Fredericton home at 177 University Avenue is more substantial. It was built from material salvaged from New Brunswick's first Government House, which was partially destroyed by fire in 1825. An indication of Saunders' concern for his creature comfort is the octagonal four-seat plastered outhouse from his country estate, now on display at Kings Landing Historical Settlement. Built in 1795, this pretentious outhouse is the Settlement's oldest structure.

Born into a wealthy Virginian planter family, Saunders inherited at an early age an estate of more than 800 acres on the east bank of the Elizabeth River in Princess Anne County: an elegant brick residence surrounded by barns, outbuildings, slave quarters, gardens, and a large orchard. Saunders' conservative views were well known and as early as 1774, he was in conflict with the rebels. Saunders supported the efforts of Governor Lord John Dunmore to suppress the rebellion. He raised a troop of cavalry at his own expense and received a captain's commission in the Queen's Own Loyal Virginia Regiment. The rebels branded Saunders a public enemy, declared him legally dead, and confiscated his property. With the Loyalist defeat at Great Bridge in December of 1776, Dunmore, Saunders, and other Virginia Loyalists fled. Saunders went to New York, where he and his troop were incorporated into the Queen's Rangers. While serving with the Rangers, Saunders was severely wounded in the flanking attack at Chadds Ford during the battle of Brandywine. Within six months he was again in action at Quinton's Bridge and Hancock's Bridge. His commander, Major John Graves Simcoe, described Saunders as an "officer of great address and determination," and selected him to lead a raid against Mamaroneck in New York. In an effort to pacify Virginia, he returned to Princess Anne County to organize the local Loyalists and establish British outposts. This attempt was short-lived, and Saunders was then appointed commander of Georgetown, South Carolina, where he became involved in the partisan struggle with rebel General Francis Marion. He remained in South Carolina until returning to New York in April, 1782. In November, 1783, he sailed to London to study law.

After being called to the bar, Saunders settled in New Brunswick where he acquired several hundred acres in the Parish of Queensbury, along the Trans-Canada Highway near Nackawic. He called his country estate "The Barony" and successfully turned to raising cattle. He married Ariana Margaretta Jekyll Chalmers, the daughter of Loyalist Lieutenant-Colonel James Chalmers, and became an important figure in the social and political life of the province, both as chief justice and as a member of the Provincial Council. John Saunders died in 1834 at the age of eighty years. His family burial plot in the Old Loyalist Burying Ground in Fredericton contains six handsome monuments, enclosed by a wrought-iron fence.

Lieutenant Samuel Denny Street of the Royal Fencible Americans

A splendid stone monument in the Old Loyalist Burying Ground in Fredericton marks the final resting place of Samuel Denny Street. He was an Englishman who had seen service in the Royal Navy and in May, 1776, enlisted as a private soldier in the Royal Fencible Americans. He served at the siege of Fort Cumberland and shortly afterwards was commissioned second lieutenant. While a member of the Fort Cumberland garrison, he married a local girl, Abigail Freeman, and together they raised twelve children. In 1781, he was stationed at Fort Howe, serving under Brigade Major Gilfred Studholme. Street had the misfortune of commanding a detachment of Fencibles on board an armed vessel that was captured by the rebels, and he was taken as prisoner to Machias, Maine. Efforts were made to parole him, but rebel Colonel John Allan reported that Street was "quite too mischievous a person to be set at liberty." Street made three attempts to escape, including one from a prison ship in Boston Harbour. He finally succeeded by escaping from a jail in Boston and swimming for over a mile up the harbour. He made his way safely back to Fort Howe, where he ended the war with the rank of lieutenant.

After being demobilized, Street studied law and settled in Burton, just south of Fredericton. He became a representative for Sunbury

County in the Legislative Assembly. He was noted for his independent stand in both the House of Assembly and in the courts, where he fought fearlessly for social justice and reform, including taking a strong antislavery position. Street's outspoken abolitionist views led to an inconclusive duel with Judge John Murray Bliss. The Honourable Samuel Denny Street died at the age seventy-nine in 1830.

Captain Caleb Jones of the Maryland Loyalists

Caleb Jones was a merchant and sheriff in Somerset County, Maryland, at the outbreak of the American Revolution. After being arrested by the rebels in 1776, Jones opted to post a bond of £200 to regain his freedom; he then decided to forfeit the bond and fled to New York, leaving his wife and son in the care of his in-laws. In December, 1777, Jones obtained a commission as a captain in the Maryland Loyalists. He served with this regiment in Philadelphia, New York, Jamaica in the West Indies, and at the siege of Pensacola, West Florida.

Along with other members of the Maryland Loyalists, Jones settled in New Brunswick near Fredericton. Within four years, by purchasing adjoining lots, he had amassed about 900 acres, beginning at the Nashwaaksis Stream and stretching down the St. John River for a mile. Having secured his land, Jones returned to Maryland to collect his family and possessions. Upon arrival, he was immediately arrested, fined, and expelled without either his family or possessions. He had left his New Brunswick property in the charge of his slaves, but on his return he was dismayed to find that his slaves had fled. In October, 1786, Jones advertised in the *Royal Gazette* that four of his slaves had escaped, and offered a six-dollar reward for their apprehension. A year later, Jones made a second trip to Maryland and successfully brought his family away.

In 1800, Jones won notoriety when he attempted to reclaim a slave by the name of Nancy. A group opposed to slavery, led by Ward Chipman and Samuel Street, provided her with support and a legal defence. Although the ensuing court decision was inconclusive, it effectively removed the right of slave owners to regain possession of their runaway slaves. This made slavery impractical, and by 1820, the practice had disappeared in New Brunswick.

Quartermaster Daniel Morehouse of the Queen's Rangers

Daniel Morehouse was born in 1758 in Redding, Fairfield County, Connecticut, to a large extended family that had lived in America for five generations. Although the Morehouses could not be considered wealthy, they were comfortable. During the American Revolutionary War, many in Fairfield County were sympathetic to the Royalist cause, and the same was true for the Morehouse family, but only Daniel and his three brothers took an active Loyalist stand. In 1776, Morehouse was attending King's College, now called Yale, when the local rebels, aware of his conservative views, demanded that he take an oath of allegiance to the Continental Congress or pay a ten-pound fine. Morehouse, with the financial assistance of an uncle, opted to pay the fine. To his chagrin, within three months the rebels were back, imposing another ten-pound fine. When he refused to pay, they confiscated his horse, saddle, and bridle. This high-handed action was too much for Morehouse; forsaking his education, he travelled with friends secretly by night to New York City and enlisted in the Queen's Rangers as a private soldier. In 1779, he was promoted sergeant.

The house built in 1812 by Quartermaster Daniel Morehouse of the Queen's Rangers for his family. KLHS

Morehouse saw continuous action with the Rangers, including at the siege of Yorktown. In 1783, he was commissioned quartermaster; after the regiment was disbanded, this entitled him to half pay of forty pounds annually and 500 acres in recognition of his rank and service.

Along with other members of the Queen's Rangers, Morehouse received a grant in the parish of Queensbury. He worked hard to develop his land and made full use of his half pay by investing in more property and building a sawmill and a gristmill. He quickly became a community leader. Along with being active in his church, Morehouse was a school trustee, a road supervisor, a justice of the peace, and a magistrate. In the militia, he reached the rank of major. As befitted his new social position, Morehouse built a comfortable home for his family in 1812. It can now be visited at Kings Landing Historical Settlement, furnished in the style of 1820 when Morehouse was at the peak of his influence. In his sons' bedroom on the second floor there are two military drums from the American Revolutionary War; the one with the cipher "RP" (standing for "Royal Provincial") is believed to have belonged to the British Legion, and the smaller one was carried by the Guides and Pioneers.

Captain Nehemiah Marks of the Armed Boatmen

In May, 1784, Captain Nehemiah Marks landed with 280 followers on the banks of the St. Croix River, hoisted the British flag, and set about establishing a new community called St. Stephen. A total of 19,850 acres was distributed to this group of Loyalists.

Marks was the son of a prominent merchant in Derby, Connecticut. Soon after the British returned to New York in October, 1776, he was employed as a "dispatch agent." Based on Long Island, he made regular clandestine crossings to Stamford and other points along the Connecticut coast, spying, collecting intelligence, and carrying dispatches. He warned of impending attacks, reported the movement of French troops, and helped to thwart rebel spies. In 1781, Marks was commissioned captain in a provincial corps called the Armed Boatmen. These men were employed as marines in whaleboats and other armed vessels, mainly in the waters around New York and Long Island. Captain Marks, who received land grants in both St. Andrews and St. Stephen, was appointed a justice of the peace, and died in St. Stephen in July, 1799.

Lieutenant Hugh McKay of the Queen's Rangers

A prominent memorial marks the final resting place of Lieutenant Hugh McKay in the cemetery next to the new Anglican Church on St. George's main street. McKay was commissioned into the Queen's Rangers as an ensign in May, 1778, and promoted lieutenant in October, 1779. He served throughout the war and was in Captain Stairs Agnew's company at the surrender of Yorktown. In 1783, he settled in St. George on half pay and became a leading citizen of Charlotte County, with a very successful milling and lumbering business. For over thirty years, he was a member of the Legislative Assembly, a colonel in the militia, and a senior judge of the Court of Common Pleas. He died at the age of ninety-seven in 1843.

42nd Highland Regiment Memorial Cemetery

The provincial historic site of the 42nd Highland Regiment Memorial Cemetery is located at Pleasant Valley on Highway 8, halfway between Taymouth and Nashwaak Bridge. The 42nd Regiment, more widely known as the Black Watch, is the oldest and most senior Highland regiment in the British Regular Army. After serving in North America during the Seven Years War, the 42nd returned in the spring of 1776 to participate in the American Revolutionary War. The regi-ment saw considerable action, including the battles of Harlem Heights, White Plains, and Brandywine. The Black Watch was one of the three battalions that made a daring night attack "with bayonet alone" at Paoli Tavern. The 42nd spent the end of the war as part of the New York garrison, and was tasked with protecting the Loyalist evacuation. It was among the last of the British troops to leave New York City.

Before returning to Britain, members of the regiment were offered the opportunity to take their discharge in North America. A return, dated September 19, 1783, shows that 181 men, thirty-five women, and thirty-five children took advantage of this offer and were embarked at New York for the St. John River Valley. They spent the winter in Saint John, while Lieutenant Dugald Campbell surveyed their grant and planned their settlement. The Highland grant was located in the parish of St. Mary's on both sides of the Nashwaak River from the Tay River to Cross Creek. It consisted of 11,343 acres, divided into 185 lots. The original map, drawn by Dugald Campbell, records that one com-missioned officer, twenty-one non-commissioned officers and drummers, ninety privates, and twenty-seven women were allotted land within the grant. The names of the settlers appear on a cairn located in the cemetery and many of them are interred there.

MacDonald Farm Provincial Historic Park

On Highway 11, west of the Bartibog Bridge, near the junction of the Miramichi and Bartibog Rivers in Northumberland County, stands the large Scottish-Georgian style masonry house built by Alexander MacDonald sometime between 1815 and 1825.

MacDonald had been a British regular soldier, serving as a private soldier in Captain McKay's Company of the 76th Regiment, also known as the Macdonald's Highlanders. The 76th was one of twelve new British regular regiments formed in response to the surrender of the British Army under General Burgoyne at Saratoga and the entrance of France into the conflict. Lord Macdonald of Sleat raised this clan regiment by recruiting from among those who were bound by tradition and ancient loyalty to follow their chief. Alexander

MacDonald, born in Argyllshire, Scotland, enlisted at age fifteen or sixteen and was one of 1,076 soldiers on strength of the regiment. The 76th was first sent to the relief of Jersey, in the English Channel, which was under attack by the French. By September, 1779, it was in North America as part of the New York garrison. In 1781, the regiment was sent as reinforcements to General Cornwallis in Virginia and was with him at the surrender of Yorktown. The regiment was disbanded in 1783, with 137 men requesting to take their discharge in Nova Scotia. MacDonald and a comrade named Angus McInnes were two of the soldiers demobilized in Shelburne in November. In the summer of 1784, the two friends travelled to the Miramichi and squatted on un-occupied land. A couple of years later they applied for and received legal title to their neighbouring lots. Alexander MacDonald eventually acquired both lots, married Grace MacLean in 1790, and built his sturdy two-and-a-half-storey home. Within fourteen years MacDonald had gone from a squatter to the owner of 450 acres. He also led an active public life, being at various times town clerk, foreman of the grand jury, commissioner, surveyor of roads, overseer of the poor, assessor, school trustee, and harbour master. He was given command of a company in the 1st Battalion, Northumberland County Militia, with the rank of captain, and eventually commanded the battalion with the rank of lieutenant-colonel. MacDonald's family grew to thirteen children, with "Gracey" having, on average, one child every fourteen months until 1815. A daughter died at age twenty-three, and an eight-year-old son was killed upstairs in the house when lightning struck the chimney. The repairs to the chimney are still discernible. MacDonald died in December, 1834 at the age of seventy-two.

Commodore George Walker and his Trading and Fishing Establishment

A provincial historical plaque at Allyson Point, near Bathurst, marks the location of an extensive trading and fishing establishment operated by Commodore George Walker from 1768 to 1778. His holding was described as "a splendid and elegantly furnished summer residence, also five large stores, a requisite number of outhouses and a tolerably strong battery." It also boasted a very fine lawn and a handsome garden. At Youghall, near the head of the harbour, Walker owned another large house which he occupied in winter, as well as a fishing establishment "on the Big River about three miles from the entrance."

Walker began his life as a mariner in the Dutch Navy, where he encountered Turkish and Greek pirates in the Mediterranean Sea. He went on to own and command merchant vessels trading with North America. Walker made his mark, however, as a privateer in the various wars of the early eighteenth century, fighting both the Spanish and the French. He became the most famous and successful British privateer of his day, but with the end of the Seven Years War, Walker had to find a more peaceful occupation and established a trading and fishing enterprise in the Bay of Chaleur. Ironically, privateers would be his undoing. With the start of the American Revolutionary War, rebel privateers swarmed into the waters of Nova Scotia and the Gulf of St. Lawrence in search of plunder. During the first two years of the conflict, Walker managed to protect his enterprise, but in July, 1778, while he was absent in England, his establishment was totally destroyed by rebel privateers. Walker died soon afterwards, and his venture was never rebuilt.

CHRONOLOGY

April 19, 1775	Battles of Lexington and Concord
April 1775 - March 1776	Siege of Boston
August 1775	Rebel privateers destroy Fort Frederick
August - November 1775	Rebel invasion of Quebec city
September - December 1775	Benedict Arnold's March to Quebec
October 1775	Royal Fencible Americans and Royal Highland Emigrants arrive in Halifax
March 17, 1776	British evacuate Boston
May 1776	Rebel privateers visit Maugerville
May 14, 1776	Maugerville declared part of Massachusetts
June 4, 1776	Goreham and Royal Fencible Americans arrive at Fort Cumberland
August 22, 1776	British invade Long Island
October 16, 1776	Battle of White Plains
November 10, 1776	Eddy demands surrender of Fort Cumberland
November 12, 1776	Rebel night assault on Fort Cumberland
November 21, 1776	Second rebel assault on Fort Cumberland
November 29, 1776	Rebels defeated and flee Fort Cumberland
April 25-28, 1777	British raid Danbury, Connecticut
May 1777	Colonel Goold on HMS *Vulture* visits St. John River Valley
June 1, 1777	Rebels under Allan capture Portland Point
June 30, 1777	British retake Portland Point
September 11, 1777	Battle of Brandywine
October 4, 1777	Battle of Germantown
October 6, 1777	British capture Forts Clinton and Montgomery

November 1777	Studholme commences construction of Fort Howe
February 6, 1778	Alliance between Congress and France prepared for signature
August 1778	Siege of Newport, Rhode Island
August 28, 1778	Battle of Quaker Hill
December 29, 1778	British capture Savannah, Georgia
June 16, 1779	Spain declares war on Britain
June 17, 1779	British occupy Castine, Maine
July 5 - 11, 1779	Tryon raids the Connecticut coast
September 12 - October 9, 1779	French and rebels besiege Savannah
May 12, 1780	British capture Charleston, South Carolina
May 29, 1780	Battle of Waxhaws
July 1, 1780	British capture Georgetown, South Carolina
August 6, 1780	Battle of Hanging Rock
August 16, 1780	Battle of Camden
October 7, 1780	Battle of King's Mountain
December 20, 1780	Britain declares war on the Netherlands
January 1781	Arnold raids James River in Virginia
March 15, 1781	Battle of Guilford Court House
April 25, 1781	Battle of Hobkirk's Hill
March - May 1781	Siege of Pensacola, East Florida
May 1781	Siege of Fort Ninety-Six
September 8, 1781	Battle of Eutaw Springs
September 12, 1781	Fanning captures Hillsborough and governor of North Carolina
September 1781	Arnold raids Connecticut coast
October 19, 1781	Surrender of Yorktown
May 11, 1783	Spring fleet arrives in Saint John
June 29, 1783	Summer fleet arrives in Saint John
September 3, 1783	Treaty of Paris
October 1, 1783	Fall fleet arrives in Saint John
November 25, 1783	British evacuate New York City
May 1784	Marks and his party arrive on St. Croix River
June 18, 1784	Creation of New Brunswick

SELECTED BIBLIOGRAPHY

ALLEN, ROBERT S., general editor. *The Loyal Americans: The Military Role of the Loyalist Provincial Corps and Their Settlement in British North America, 1775 - 1784*. Ottawa: National Museum of Man, 1983.

And the River Rolled On: Two Hundred Years on the Nashwaak. Fredericton: Nashwaak Bicentennial Association, 1984.

BAKELESS, JOHN. *Turncoats, Traitors and Heroes: Espionage in the American Revolution*. New York: Da Capo, 1998.

BATES, WALTER. *Kingston and the Loyalists of the "Spring Fleet" of 1783*. Rpt. Fredericton: Non-Entity, 1980.

BUNNELL, PAUL J. *Thunder over New England: Benjamin Bonnell, the Loyalist*. Norwell, MA: Christopher Publishing House, 1988.

_____. *The New Loyalist Index, Volumes I, II, and III*. Bowie, MD: Heritage, 1996.

CLARKE, ERNEST. *The Siege of Fort Cumberland, 1776: An Episode in the American Revolution*. Montreal and Kingston: McGill-Queen's University Press, 1995.

CONDON, ANN GORMAN. *The Loyalist Dream for New Brunswick*. Fredericton: New Ireland, 1984.

CURTIS, EDWARD E. *The Organization of the British Army in the American Revolution*. Rpt. East Ardsley, Yorkshire: ER Publishing, 1972.

DUBEAU, SHARON. *New Brunswick Loyalists: A Bicentennial Tribute*. Agincourt, ON: Generation, 1983.

FINLEY, A. GREGG. *The Loyalists: A Catalogue Featuring Selected Pieces of Loyalist History from the Collections of the New Brunswick Museum*. Saint John: New Brunswick Museum, 1975.

FRYER, MARY BEACOCK. *Allan Maclean Jacobite General*. Toronto: Dundurn, 1987.

HARGREAVES, REGINALD. *The Bloodybacks: The British Serviceman in North America and the Caribbean 1655 - 1783*. London: Rupert Hart-Davies, 1968.

HEBB, ROSS N. *Quaco St. Martins*. Fredericton: Quaco/Springhill, 1997.

HILL, ISABEL LOUISE. *The Old Burying Ground Fredericton, N.B. Volumes I and III*. Fredericton: Fredericton Heritage Trust, 1981.

LEAMON, JAMES S. *Revolution Downeast: The War for American Independence in Maine*. Amherst: University of Massachusetts, 1993.

MacDONALD, M.A. *Rebels & Royalists: The Lives and Material Culture of New Brunswick's Early English-Speaking Settlers, 1758 - 1783*. Fredericton: New Ireland, 1990.

MacNUTT, W.S. *The Atlantic Provinces: The Emergence of Colonial Society, 1712-1857*. Toronto: McClelland and Stewart, 1965.

POTTER-MacKINNON, JANICE. *While the Women Only Wept: Loyalist Refugee Women in Eastern Ontario*. Montreal and Kingston: McGill-Queen's University Press, 1993.

REES, RONALD. *Land of the Loyalists: Their Struggle to Shape the Maritimes*. Halifax: Nimbus, 2000.

THOMAS, EARLE. *Greener Pastures: The Loyalist Experience of Benjamin Ingraham*. Belleville, ON: Mika, 1983.

VINCENT, G.R. *The Civil Sword: James Delancey's Westchester Refugees*. Victoria: Cobequid, 2000.

WRIGHT, ESTHER CLARKE. *The Loyalists of New Brunswick*. Hantsport NS: Lancelot, 1981.

INDEX

NEW BRUNSWICK MILITARY HERITAGE PROJECT

The New Brunswick Military Heritage Project, a non-profit organization devoted to public awareness of the remarkable military heritage of the province, is an initiative of the Military and Strategic Studies Program of the University of New Brunswick. The organization consists of museum professionals, teachers, university professors, graduate students, active and retired members of the Canadian armed forces, and other historians. We welcome public involvement. People who have ideas for books or information for our database can contact us through our Web site: www.unb.ca/nbmhp.

One of the main activities of the New Brunswick Military Heritage Project is the publication of the New Brunswick Military Heritage Series with Goose Lane Editions. This series of books is under the direction of Marc Milner, Director of the Military and Strategic Studies Program, and J. Brent Wilson, Research Director of the Centre for Conflict Sudies, both at the University of New Brunswick. Publication of the series is supported by a grant from the Canadian War Musuem.

ABOUT THE AUTHOR

Robert Leonard Dallison attended both the Royal Roads Military College and the Royal Military College, and following graduation in 1958, was commissioned lieutenant in the Princess Patricia's Canadian Light Infantry. Prior to joining his regiment he completed a B.A. (History and International Studies) at the University of British Columbia. He served for thirty-five years with the Canadian Army, obtaining the rank of lieutenant-colonel. In addition to serving in both the 1st and 2nd Battalions of the PPCLI, he was seconded to the Ghanian Army in West Africa for two years; was a tactics instructor at the School of Infantry; attended the Canadian Army Staff College; did a tour of duty with the United Nations in Cyprus; was an intelligence staff officer in Central Army Group Headquarters in Heidelberg, Germany; commanded the PPCLI Battle School for three years; and ended his career as Chief of Staff of the Combat Arms School at CFB Gagetown. After retiring from the Canadian Army, he maintained his lifelong interest in history and heritage, including serving as the President of Fredericton Heritage Trust, and, for six years, as the New Brunswick representative on the Board of Governors for Heritage Canada. From 1992 to 2002, he was Director of Kings Landing Historical Settlement.